CURRICULUM TRADITIONS AND PRACTICES

Donald K. Sharpes

ST. MARTIN'S PRESS
New York

First published in the United States of America in 1988

Printed in Great Britain

ISBN 0-312-02086-4

LC 88-42605
Library of Congress Cataloging-in-Publication Data applied for.

70
518
88

Contents

Contents

Acknowledgements

It pleases me to acknowledge my debt to all those who influenced my thinking about curriculum and learning, and those who contributed significantly to the production of this book.

First, my instructors. I want to thank Lee Cronbach, Nate Gage, Dwight Allen, Fred McDonald, Ernest Hilgard, Richard Atkinson, Ralph Tyler, Arnold Toynbee, George Spindler and Nelson Haggerson.

I owe a special thanks to certain colleagues who, in discussions, have influenced my thinking, including: Dave Berliner, Jerome Bruner, Lloyd Trump, Mal Provus, Don Davies, Louis Rubin, Fen English, John Goodlad, Wayne Worner, Dick Jones, John Oxenham, Jud Taylor, Michael Apple, Mortimer Adler, Karl Hereford, John Gardner, Michael Scriven, Don Bigelow, Harold Howe, B.O. Smith, Gerald Firth, Jim Olivero, Richard Graham. In many cases I have also profited from the reading of these same colleagues, and their references may also be cited in the bibliography.

I owe thanks to my former employers--Stanford University, Arizona State University, the U.S. Office of Education (now the U.S. Department of Education), Virginia Polytechnic Institute and State University, and to my present institutional affiliation, Weber State College and Utah State University's combined graduate program.

I have of course benifitted from my six years of secondary school teaching experience and my service as an Assistant Principal and Acting Principal in drawing on curriculum development experiences. Without naming them all, I have served as a consultant to over 75 schools and school systems, several state education agencies, scores of colleges and universities, about a dozen overseas higher education institutions, and three foreign government ministries of education.

I am grateful to the production team, especially David Croom and Sue Joshua at Croom Helm Publishers, and Naomi Roth, formerly at Croom Helm and now at Open University Press, and to Julia Christmas who aided in the preparation of the manuscript, and the production staff at the Weber State College Printing Office.

To the over 1000 graduate students in curriculum and foundations who have benefitted from my instruction, thank you for challenging my concepts and questioning my strategies.

I would like to extend my thanks to the following book publishers, journals and magazines for permission to quote from passages or refer to articles. In chapter two, Adler's the *Paideia Proposal*, from Macmillan Publishers. In chapter four, Goodlad's *A Place Called School*, from McGraw Hill; Taba's *Curriculum Development*, from Harcourt, Brace & Jovanovich; and Tyler's *Basic Principles of Curriculum and Instruction*, from the University of Chicago Press. In chapter five, "Federal Education for the American Indian," from the *Journal of American Indian Education*; and "A Curiculum Model," from the *Journal of American Indian Education*. In chapter six, "A Developmental Curriculum for the Mildly Retarded of Intermediate and High School Age," from *Education and Training of the Mildly Retarded*. In chapter eight, "Have A Discipline Problem? Turn to Your Community for Help in Schools," from the *American School Board Journal*. And in chapter ten, "Incentive Pay and the Promotion of Teaching Proficiencies," from *The Clearing House*.

PART ONE:

CURRICULUM TRADITIONS

The time will come when diligent research over long time
will bring to light things which now lie hidden...knowledge
will be unfolded only through long successive ages. There
will come a time when our descendants will be amazed that
we did not know things that are so plain to them...our
universe is a sorry little affair unless it has in it something
for every age to investigate.

Seneca, *Natural Questions*
Book 7

Introduction

> Grammar, the ground of all teaching
> now baffles girls and boys;
> not one of our new learners today
> takes pain enough
> to write correct verses
> or compose a competent letter.

William Langland, PIERS PLOWMAN
(c. 1370)

Curriculum, rather than helping define the nature and scope of schooling, has itself become a problem of definition. The standard text on curriculum has traditionally used schooling subjects to define the curriculum arena, or describe activities in the field. School personnel typically think of curriculum as English, math, science, social studies, foreign languages, art and music, and so on. The program of studies for students has embraced what educators believe they should teach in a classroom, and what students should learn from texts.

This understanding, derived in part from the long illustrious legacy of the liberal arts, and in part from the formalization of programs of studies as schooling expanded to include all youth, has been consistently challenged in this century by both the numerical increase of formal education everywhere in the world and the accessibility of schooling. But large student populations demand more flexibile curriculum responses, not more uniformity. Moreover, students who in previous generations have been denied admission to schooling now seek extended schooling opportunities. Thus, girls, the working class, the handicapped--to name a few--have in recent years been allowed to participate in the benefits of schooling.

Where schooling was once private, with the expansion of industrialization, it has become public. However, the general outline of the program of studies, the curriculum, has not altered appreciably. The curriculum has persisted in form and content and remains relatively unchanged.

In fact, as schooling expanded in the developing world the industrialized western model of schooling was exported as one of the more desirable commodities. As former colonies and new independent countries acquired the structure of schooling, they also imported the same curriculum content...in many cases the same textbooks. When it became apparent that the liberal arts as understood did not necessarily help

3

resolve the problems of subsistence agriculture, the balance of payments, foreign trade, or any of the identified problems of national development, vocational schools, with the assistance of World Bank loans, became the alternative curriculum model for formal education.

The changing work conditions in the modern age should bring about some change in vocational attitudes towards the actual and potential job market. Thus, vocational programs should not be just training for specific occupations, but career orientations for a volatile and unpredictable labor force. Vocational programs--too often viewed as a poor man's substitute to the "academics" curriculum--should be a part of general education. They have varied little because the ideology for preparing students for the work environment has varied little. It is no longer feasible to expect schools actually to prepare students for long-term meaningful occupations as it once was. The hope has to be that schools orient students to a changing job climate in which, unless they choose a profession, there will be substantive technological advances that will alter jobs and hiring patterns. Vocational curricula also need flexibility in conception and execution.

Unlike medicine or science, where new experiments can dramatically improve life, experiments in curriculum that prepare people for adult intellectual life are generally viewed with suspicion. Under some social pressure, a new curriculum model may be temporarily installed. When it does not immediately improve school conditions, or improve gain scores in student achievement, or satisfy teachers, authorities revert quickly to the former complacency of the traditional design. The traditional curriculum is safe, everyone seems to understand it, and it does not require uncomfortable adjustments.

Schools teach science, but they do not do science. They do not experiment with new ways for improving both the content and the delivery of the knowledge services. Few educators see the inconsistency in teaching the importance of the modern scientific method, and the lack of its application to the curriculum and schooling process. It is not necessary that schools also be research organizations. But it is important that schools be the place where validated experiments can be practiced. The curriculum has assumed a kind of dogmatic dignity, because schools do not experiment with curriculum. If the curriculum portends to be the heart of what civilization knows about its past, all available evidence points to the conclusion that graduates of secondary schools are less literate and knowledgeable than previous generations. Students today may be more ignorant about who they are, where they come from, what the world is, and where they are going than ever before. The evidence for this is distressing in the extreme. Schools may be losing the war against ignorance.

The uncertainty principle in physics is that you cannot know a subatomic particle's position and momentum at the same time. What is certain now is that fewer students understand the uncertainty principle. It took Socrates a lifetime to understand how ignorant he was. The present generation has made extraordinary progress by realizing its own ignorance much earlier on.

The causes for this malaise are manifold. Part of the reason is our compulsion to remedy past generations' unequal access to formal schooling. Mandatory attendance laws, coupled with a chic attitude among students not to care about what they learn, have refocused teaching activities on classroom management and control behaviors. Students (it might be more accurate to classify many as simply attendees) who a few years ago would not have been in school at all are now forced to remain until a certain age. The maintenance in schools of many students who do not choose to be there has noticeably reduced the average standardized test scores in achievement compared with just a few years ago.

The post-World War II population expansion in the industrialized world created unprecedented numbers of students and teaching positions. Teachers poured into the training colleges and universities. The quality of their preparation came into question, as did the quality of the candidates themselves relative to students in other academic pursuits. The explosion of programs, schools, students and teachers in the 1960s, and the diminution of teaching quality, created a negative influence on overall student achievement, and the beginnings of complaints from the body politic.

Knowledge, as the educated Western person understands it, is fading from the culture for both a lack of interest and faulty transmission. So, although one of the purposes of this book is to trace the historical and philosophical foundations of Western intellectual tradition in curriculum in a brief summary, and to demonstrate some examples of how educators can design curriculum programs for specific student populations, I also want to point out the much larger dimension of where curriculum fits in the schooling context. It is an unfavorable outlook. At a time crucial to the maintenance of democratic principles and government, many teachers are impoverished intellectually. As a society we have entrusted them with the responsibility of passing on the best of civilized thought. Many teachers don't teach the basics of culture because they don't know them.

The overall decline in gain scores in student achievement is indicative of a congeries of causes, only one of which is a decline in teaching quality. Salaries commensurate with the societal responsibility, and with other professions, are still in retreat. The causal relationship of achievement gain scores on standardized tests to curriculum will always be a tenuous understanding. There are too many powerful intervening variables to establish a firm link. Among them are genetic influences, whose combination with environmental influences will always be hotly contested. What is clear is that gifted and talented students will always perform well compared with other students in the formal curriculum. It is equally clear from published evidence that intellectually deficient students can do remarkably well if sufficient teacher time is spent assisting their studies. In sum, the teacher variable is the most significant influence on student learning. In a sense, the curriculum is neutral.

And yet when the transmission of knowledge to youth is in dangerous decline, the so-called information age has arrived. The number of people involved as professionals in the knowledge business has increased. In the U.S. in 1960, professionals accounted for 7.5 million and 11 percent of the work force. In 1981, the number was 16.4 million and constituted 17 percent of all workers.

Knowledge is indeed the new critical element in the modern age, and the driving force behind the new technologies and economies. The difference here, for schools and the curriculum, is that by and large the enormous pool of knowledge does not exist in schools, nor in the curriculum. It exists outside the schools.

Consequently, schools, and by implication the curriculum, however much we may re-arrange their parts, beautify them, make their objectives more specific, quantify their evaluations, publish their test results, are still only modest agents of the enculturation process. What schools now seem to reflect is an unenviable status of mediocrity vis-à-vis the total world of the knowledge industry and its transmission of new discoveries. For the average citizen, the culture itself may be in flight.

Whole regions of America, and especially large portions of its youth, have never known its cultural roots, and have neglected or never learned the forms of intellectual inquiry that have shaped civilized life. This is

5

not meant to be a universal indictment but a perception based on wide experience and analysis. Schools may not be the proper forum for cultural reform. By default, schools have lost the role as principal agency for knowledge transmission to the media, whose primary objective in the U.S. is entertainment and the advertisement of consumer products.

Schools, of all social agencies, are the most conservative. Perhaps only the new international heroes and heroines--the rock stars, cinema celebrities and athletic contestants--can have an impact. The limited decline in use of harmful drugs is attributable to athletes appearing on television to speak against their use. We are in danger of losing even myths and caricature as cultural elements as we promote entertainment and athletic events.

Another purpose of this book is to demonstrate a multiple approach to curriculum development based on the social and behavioral sciences. The first section is a clear example of the historical relevancy of philosophy, its legacy and methodology, to the development of schooling questions will always be an appropriate methodology, either for formulating curriculum or learning objectives, or as an instructional technique. Philosophy is the grandfather of most of the sciences, and certainly the progenitor of psychology.

Similarly, the chapter using an example of a homogeneously ethnic student population based on the American Indian is an effort to use the strategies of cultural anthropology in curriculum design. The use of ethnography, for example, as a methodology for understanding schooling activities has been on the rise. My purpose in this chapter is to re-conceptualize, from a given cultural extension of cultural foundations and understandings. This process has already occurred in many developing countries which have modified the developed world's curricula to the indigenous culture.

The chapter illustrating a sample design for a curriculum for the mildly retarded is built upon the principles of developmental psychology. Although the chief concepts are embedded in the assumptions, this chapter offers some useful survey instruments for a curriculum oriented to vocational skills and job opportunities.

The sample curriculum for the physically handicapped is also an example of an action plan based on developmental psychology and offers a very detailed set of student learning objectives. The emphasis here is less on the cognitive skills required and more on the social and emotional development associated with the child's physical disability--in many cases multiple disabilities. There is a certain amount of normal trauma connected with going to school. But for children and youth who also carry the burden of physical and mental handicaps, the psychological and social developmental rites of passage are magnified during the schooling years. This curriculum design speaks to that necessary component usually missing from the curriculum.

In the same way, I attempted to re-formulate an appropriate schema for a curriculum for disruptive students based on meanings from sociology. The point in each of these curriculum examples is not to imitate slavishly a textbook design of what psychology, sociology, or cultural anthropology is, but to transfer a gestalt of the discipline to constructing a curriculum plan. I believe that curriculum, as a planning exercise for delivering knowledge, should actively borrow both the theoretical constructs and methodologies of the social and behavioral sciences.

The curriculum examples in the second part of this book are meant to emphasize the diagnosis of student needs as one of the principal beginning elements in curriculum development. The structure of academic disciplines has a concrete history and definition. But curriculum does not have a response to a student who says, "I hate math," or science or poetry. The teacher--or curriculum--must intervene with a different kind of response, appropriate to temperament and specificity of purpose: to reach the student first, and then to inform.

I believe that there is always an emotional response to the curriculum from students: love or hate at the extremes, and intermediate stages in between. Teachers, regardless of the plan of studies, need to address this emotional reaction, not with defensive posturing, but with a unit that aids social and emotional development. Consequently, teaching for social and emotional growth becomes the primary objective irrespective of subject taught at certain points in the continuum of learning.

My argument is that curriculum can be a flexible response to both content and process a re-fashioning of how we consider what students are to learn, and the manner in which they learn it. This is not meant to be a compromise on academic integrity of any subject. It is meant to be an accommodation of the under-rated degree of student interest, culture, level of readiness or academic preparation, and biological development towards mastering a discipline, or even learning the rudiments.

Something called a "core" curiculum has been in vogue for many years. The term has been used to describe both a core of matter within a subject, and a core for general education, a sort of national curriculum. The U.S. does not have a national system of education, although there is surprising uniformity of curricular offerings even in the absence of a national mandate and system of governance. However, most industrialized countries do have a national system, and many, like the United Kingdom in the late 1980's, faced the prospect of a national debate on the contents of a standard curriculum for all schools. The U.K.'s plan consisted of English, maths, science, foreign languages, history, geography and technology. Critics argued that absent were moral values and skills such as reading and writing.

Another approach to a core curriculum of recent origin is simply a block of time within a schedule. In this instance, the organization of schooling has corrupted the legitimacy of a useful concept based on common student interest and a broader interpretation of subject matter. The uniform time schedule standardizes the curriculum by assuming all subjects are of equal importance. The school schedule is an administrative convenience that by its uniformity ignores the variability of student learning rates and progress

The core curriculum, although it had its excessive advocates at one time, was at the heart (the root meaning of the term "core" a way to provide students with common encounters of the most significant and representative levels of human experience.

Clearly, a society must be able to specify what it wants its young to know. The political dimension of curriculum development will always be a topical concept and relevant factor. There are signs that the political activists at governmental levels, in response to vocal public demands, are shaping the policies of curriculum reform in statutes and public pronouncements.

For example, in 1986 the U.S. Department of Education released a publication called *What Works: Research About Teaching and Learning.* It was an expression, as Gene Glass reminds us, of conservative political philosophy and not a consensus of research findings found to be successful. The document sought to disestablish federal control, and diminish federal financial support. It argued that the results of educational research were already confirmed by reading the great thinkers in the liberal arts tradition, and what was likely common sense, and distinctly played down the important role of scientific investigation in schooling practices. This single 65-page publication simultaneously gave wide circulation to the conservative ideology of the Reagan Administration, and gave short shrift to the whole body of educational research in the past few decades and to the process of federal participation in schooling research. The lesson here is that the political machinery will use education, schooling, research or curriculum to its own ideological ends. Scientific facts may not always compel government action.

Despite often large-scale investment and expectation, few curriculum innovations find their way into adopted practice. Government intervention in curriculum development never seems to transcend the pilot project phase. This is even more true in developing countries, and the World Bank reports on the thwarting of and active resistance to curriculum change by poorly informed school personnel, and by inadequate resources, poor strategies for implementing designs, and insufficient attention to monitoring.

The role of curriculum development in developing countries, which often established their own development centers, was usually adaptation to the indigenous culture. Content was usually modified for local consumption without questioning new instructional techniques, or conventional wisdom about the nature of academic subject matter. By the late 1970's, many countries had these locally adapted curriculum units in use. But some disillusionment set in as the goals of nationalistic sentiment subsided, and as the costs of national curriculum intervention, particularly in science, increased. Thus, curriculum also fell victim to the global recession and the high costs of importing energy.

The economic dimension of curriculum development is also central to understanding how curricula get done in schools. Global recession, currency fluctuations, imbalances in trade, the lowering of prices for mineral resources (excluding oil)--all contribute to budget restraints in curriculum development in both the developing and industrialized world. The low rates of economic growth, when associated with significant population increases in the developing world, lead to very real declines in expenditures per pupil.

These imbalances in educational services often get translated into less salary money. In essence, this often means more inexperienced teachers; an increase in the pupil-teacher ratio; a disproportion of teacher pay compared to other positions in the labor force; more temporary teachers. All these combined factors influence the amount and quality of curriculum development that can be accomplished within a nation, a district, a school.

In addition to external factors, I believe that the quality of the combined services within a school can influence the way in which school personnel approach curriculum improvement. In other words if the political and economic conditions of curricular reform are demanding, the bureaucratic constraints can be inertia personified. It is the conformity of the existing orthodoxy of how schools manage the total program which can inhibit vital changes in curriculum. Among these administrative provisions are: the school's time schedule; the teacher salary schedule; the uniformity of instructional strategies; the use of facilities (as in standard classroom size); the dominance of formal subjects as the only legitimate curriculum model.

According to John Goodlad and his studies of schooling, 88 percent of instructional time in secondary schools is taken up with telling, questioning the whole class, monitoring seatwork, and doing quizzes. The evidence points to standardization in curriculum, and an emphasis on direct instructional techniques.

In the final analysis, curriculum does not stand in lovely isolation, waiting only a cosmetic face-lift, a repair and tune-up to set it on its way. It is really only a concept--the concept of the practice of teaching as I view it--that must work in concert with other elements in the formal organization to achieve its ultimate purposes of cultural transmission and socialization of the young. The curriculum is not an end in itself, but a manipulative tool, like any other device, used to attain educational goals.

Chapter One

A POINT OF DEPARTURE FOR A CURRICULUM DEFINITION

DEFINING CURRICULUM

The root meaning of the word curriculum comes from the Latin *currere*, to run, and refers to the Roman races, sometimes done with horses and chariots, and often in dangerous and life-threatening conditions. Some students may feel that schooling, like running a Roman race course, is equally menacing. But in industrialized societies more than ninety percent complete secondary schooling without serious health impairments.

Curriculum writers and theorists are searching for meaning in the study of curriculum through definition. Curriculum has been defined as both content and process, as what is taught in schools, and as the process of deciding what to teach. Other cultural and social determinants are frequently described under the unhelpful genre of "the hidden curriculum," or as "sources" or " conceptions." It is an unfortunate state for an intellectual pursuit when few can agree on what constitutes the boundaries of the quest.

Definitions range from a written plan to the whole schooling process. The curriculum is a document; a syllabus; a process for developing a plan; it is the plan and the execution; it is a system; it is the structure of an undefined discipline. Its real meaning can only be found in social science concepts: society, culture, the nature of knowledge. Phrases like "planned learning experiences," or "a structured series of intended learning outcomes," emphasize either planning or teaching for what the student learns.

Curriculum, moreover, is often understood as synonymous with the organization of the delivery of knowledge: the planning to teach. Schooling knowledge closely parallels the academic disciplines. Curriculum is thus transmitted through the levels of schooling--primary, elementary and secondary--by loosely defined age and grade levels.

At one extreme, the curriculum is what is contained in school textbooks, with additions or deletions regulated by governmental agencies. Domains of social consideration also assume curricular importance, like safety, sex, drug abuse or multicultural education. But in general, the textbook industry, the mandates of government intervention, the organization of the schools, all determine the curriculum, and fix, seemingly unalterably, the curriculum content and process.

Curriculum writers have conceptually separated what a teacher does from what is written. But what if there were no books in school at all? What is the curriculum under such a condition? Like the medieval alchemist, we are in a vain search for a substance which must be fired in a different kind of crucible.

If the curriculum were confined merely to written material, there would be no need for teachers. Schools would hypothetically only need to teach reading, pass out documents, and test for the results. Schooling is obviously more than this; therefore, the curriculum must include the teacher in its definition.

I define curriculum as the teaching act. In this definition, the curriculum is not a plan, but the plan in action. The curriculum is not a body of knowledge, but someone knowing what to teach. This implies that curriculum is what the teacher does, and what the teacher knows, and who the teacher is: the teacher's behavior, knowledge and personality. Instruction, how the teacher teaches, is one side of the coin; curriculum, what the teacher teaches, is the other.

The study of the curriculum, however defined, is definitely not a science, not a discipline in the traditional sense, and only possibly an art. It is a part of the study of formal schooling which has traditionally borrowed from other branches of knowledge--philosophy, sociology, anthropology, math and statistics--to conduct its inquiries. Curriculum has no methodology of its own.

Every experienced teacher has examples of teaching a class unprepared, as it were. And yet, often the teaching turned out to be spontaneously good, the extemporaneous encounter proceeding supposedly without a plan. But how can teaching proceed without a curriculum? Or can it be that the combined experience of a teacher, brought to bear in an actual teaching act, is, after all, the curriculum? I believe that it is, and that the leaning of the working definitions about the curriculum towards lesson plans is a mis-directed study focus which ignores the crucial role of the teacher in the teaching, not the planning act.

Consider the case of Socrates, revered by educators, and whose phrase "know thyself" is much quoted as an example of Hellenic wisdom. Although we acknowledge his importance to western civilization, his method for eradicating ignorance is not universally followed. Socrates' first premise is that most men do not even know what knowledge they lack. The uninformed person cannot give acceptable reasons for assumed knowledge. The first step is to let the individual see how little he understands, and to create a condition of perplexity and doubt. The last step is for the individual (and here read, student) to reconstruct experiences to justify belief.

It is continuous "dialogue" which is the essential feature of Socratic thinking. It is the opposite of didacticism, the present schooling method, much maligned but still universally practiced. Socrates emphasized the condition of doubt, not certainty. As an afterthought, he was also put to death by the Athenian authorities for corrupting youth with this method.

Now, given this Socratic method of philosophical and educational inquiry, which persisted for over 1500 years in Europe, what would be the curriculum? The plan, if you could call it one, is to eradicate ignorance. The process is one of questioning, probing, discussing, clarifying. There is no preconceived structure, no set rules governing the discussion. There are questions. Socrates at work, plying his inquisitive trade, is my example of defining the curriculum.

The lack of acceptable or purposeful theory has led curriculum workers to generate goals and objectives, plans and schemes, collections of experiences, the exposition and treatment of subjects and disciplines, even lives to be lived, without benefit of common purpose in research. A curriculum has been considered successful if it delivered and fulfilled its mission on one or more of these practical dimensions. Why then is there not a commonly accepted departure for forming a theory or even definition of curriculum from which experiments might either validate or disprove hypotheses?

Part of the difficulty stems from acceptance of simple definitions rooted in theory. The defining of a curriculum has not been absent from curriculum theory. What is missing is mutual responsiveness to a definition from which experimentation can be conducted. The irony is that curriculum theorizers are running around the professional race course from different starting pens without stop watches, finishing   lines or jockeys.

NO COMMON GROUND

James B. McDonald has perhaps stated the logjam and impasse as well as anyone. "Curriculum theory and theorizing may be characterized as being in a rather formative condition for essentially there are no generally accepted and clear-cut criteria to distinguish curriculum theory and theorizing from other forms of writing in education."(McDonald, 1975)

Bruce Joyce notes that "...the curriculum field has forced itself to operate within parameters so restrictive that it has been unable to develop strong validated theory and it has been impotent to improve education"(Joyce, 1971).

Hilda Taba seemed saddened by what she considered to be the confusion in curriculum theorizing. She characterized chiefly ways of *organizing* what was to be taught, such as the core curriculum, the broad fields curriculum, and the life experience curriculum. What she proposed and developed in her classic work, *Curriculum Development, Theory and Practice,* was a theory--not of curriculum--but of how to structure activities for learning development.

In a refreshing work, Hugh Sockett, in *Designing the Curriculum,* characterizes those who develop master plans as utopian. But he does begin his inquiry with the question of what a curriculum is and ends by saying that it is whatever any curriculum writer wants to call it. "When you say, therefore, that this is what a curriculum is, you are simply stipulating a definition: you are saying, in effect, that for my purposes I will take a curriculum to be this. For you cannot say what it is."(Sockett, 1976)

For King and Brownell "the theory of the nature of the world of intellect becomes the *model* for a theory of curriculum"(King, 1966). They state further: "There is a field of study in education termed *curriculum,* and there is a body of literature which might generously be termed *theory.* With few exceptions in the literature on curriculum, *theory* has been loosely construed, vaguely "philosophical", and by no means "scientific". Saylor and Alexander note that the curriculum is "a plan for providing sets of learning opportunities to achieve broad educational goals and related specific objectives for an identifiable population served by a single school center"(Saylor, 1974).

Philip Phenix describes, in *Realms of Meaning,* essentially a philosophy of curriculum: "...philosophy of the curriculum is necessary. By such a philosophy is meant a critically examined, coherent system of ideas by which all the constituent parts of the course of instruction are identified and ordered"(Phenix, 1964).

Many proponents, including Brownell, King and especially Phenix, believe that the disciplines themselves are the curriculum. It is true the subjects contain meaning and order, and that orderly development and disciplined thinking is the purpose for their instruction. But order and understanding do not exist apart from an understanding mind, as I will discuss momentarily.

Curriculum books for elementary and secondary schools are categorized nearly always by subjects such as vocational education or special programs like guidance. Inlow's book explores such topics as mental health in the schools, creativity and problem-solving. Yet even Inlow concedes the supremacy of the subjects or disciplines, following nearly everyone else.

Firth and Kingston define curriculum as "an all-inconclusive term with innumerable definitions" (Firth, 1973).

Bruce Joyce and Marsha Weil describe a curriculum as "an educational program" (Joyce, 1972).

William Pinar has classified the curriculum field into the work of traditionalists, conceptual-empiricists, and reconceptualists, relying on the stimulating work of Jurgen Habermas and Richard Bernstein as sources (Pinar, 1978).

George A. Beauchamp in *Curriculum Theory* was forthright enough to state that "...in spite of language used about curriculum theory, we have no identified field of curriculum theory nor any basic framework for making one... " Elsewhere he says, "The function of theory in curriculum is a topic that has been neither fully nor carefully treated in curriculum literature" (Beauchamp, 1975).

"A curriculum is a written document...but basically it is a plan for the education of pupils," states Beauchamp. In another place he notes: "Chief among the problems for the curriculum theorist, however, is the establishment of precise meanings associated with the basic concepts of curriculum...the important term for curriculum theory is *curriculum*. From a theoretical point of view, it is impossible to develop subordinate constructs, or relationships, with other components of education, until ground rules are laid down through meanings ascribed to the basic term curriculum" (Beauchamp, 1975). What makes the state of curriculum so fragmented is this universally acknowledged lack of a theory base from which to conduct research.

LEARNING THEORIES OR PHILOSOPHIES OF EDUCATION

But by and large curriculum has been descriptions of techniques for planning. Constructing the design or the plan according to a particular learning theory--for example the developmental needs of children--has constituted the bulk of what we know as curriculum theory, if in fact the learning base has been present at all. Alternative designs are said to be at work if students use different ways, like discussion and reading to satisfy a curriculum plan.

If design or development is the primary feature that distinguishes one curriculum theory from another, then I suggest that it is not a curriculum theory we are agreeing upon, but a theory of learning or philosophy of education. It is one or the other that has generally characterized curriculum theory and development.

If learning theory, like contingency management strategies, is one of the primary foundations for curriculum development, as most readily acknowledged, then the question posed repeatedly is, what is the curriculum design for out-of-school experiences? Of course there is none that satisfies curriculum theory as presently known, and the dilemma serves as yet another reminder that there is no curriculum theory apart from subject knowledge or learning theory within a schooling context.

Curriculum also presumes certain value and cultural determinations; and, as Illich maintains, "the curriculum has always been used to assign social rank..." (Illich, 1970). He believes further that "most learning happens casually, and even most intentional learning is not the result of programmed instruction."

Because of the acknowledged absence of a curriculum theory it has been natural to turn to other fields of inquiry for guidance in understanding something about the context and processes of what happens in curriculum development and transmission. John D. McNeil has noted that "Learning principles like those advocating feedback, appropriate practice, and reward, are now being dethroned as indicators of good practice" (McNeil, 1978). Anthropology, sociology, and political science have been the logical source for theoretical development. Curriculum has borrowed heavily from the behavioral and social sciences in an attempt to explain its functions.

SYSTEMS APPROACH TO CURRICULUM DEVELOPMENT

The transformation of civilized, industrialized society has made obsolete some disciplines and subjects which were not useful in solving contemporary problems. Latin is clearly one. Consequently, such programs as systems engineering, policy analysis, and operations research have become the new disciplines that prepare tomorrow's professional personnel. Such curriculum divergence has not yet fully become a part of elementary and secondary school curricula, although developers have borrowed heavily on the language if not the substance.

If there is agreement in curriculum design and development it is that the blueprint changes. Curriculum is revised because the curriculum developers do not agree on a theory. The grand design approach to curriculum development, understandably, is thus likened to the industrial-engineering model, or the systems approach.

The systems approach has led to the setting of curriculum goals and objectives, perhaps the most common form of curriculum development. What predominates as an expression of curriculum thinking is the behavioral scientist's approach to conceiving the sequencing of behavior. As a result, curriculum activities are the writing of instructional or behavioral objectives. The sources for this information come from concepts about society, the culture, learning theories, or the nature of knowledge. The trend is an attempt to redirect curriculum development away from traditional reliance on a single principle or subject like physics, English or math. The widespread acceptance of the learning needs of students, at least conceptually throughout the profession, has spurred this movement.

But the behavioral approach to curriculum development helps standardize the concept that curriculum theory is no more nor less than the design of a goals and objectives model with its attendant activities and evaluation strategies and sequence. "Curriculum theory and curriculum design are almost inextricably related," say Saylor and Alexander(1974). Curriculum, then, has not been anything more than the *writing* of the desired logical sequence of ways of learning. It is what we hope the students will learn or what the teachers might accomplish.

CURRICULUM IN THE SCHOOL STRUCTURE

Improbably and yet persistently, curriculum theory development, as opposed to the design of specific curriculums, has been *hampered by the way in which schools are organized to deliver the curriculum.* Over occasional lamentations, curricula are planned and staged in teaching subjects, fixed in time modules of uniform length, and prescribed in ritualistic fashion. The curricula have been imbedded in the school's organization, and are unrecognizable apart from that organization and the subjects which dictate their order.

Recall that in recent memory the manner of revising the curricula and rendering more flexible the alternatives for student learning was to reorganize curriculum delivery: team teaching, flexible scheduling, differentiated staffing, open spaces. The working hypothesis was that if time, staffing patterns, and organizational structure in general could be more adaptable and responsive to change in learning styles, then learning-- as an expression of understanding the curriculum--could be accelerated. Inconclusive and disjointed evidence resulted in further disillusionment, especially with the methodology controlling for the influence of the school as an organization and its changes.

Thus, rather than acting as a liberating agent, the curriculum has become a constraint. Once instituted as a plan, it becomes a part of the organizational structure of how learning is presumed to occur. Since so much has gone into its design, it cannot bear deviation without pain or anger from the logic of its order. The order of the design presumes and implies the sequence and the timing of what is to be learned.

TEACHER BEHAVIOR AS CURRICULUM

The curriculum is not a plan to be followed, but teaching behaviors to be analyzed. Consequently, curriculum is not something the teacher needs to complete, to develop in more detail, or even needs to understand. In its final form, the curriculum is not an intermediary through which learning is supposed to occur.

I purposefully omit what the student can learn without the teacher or from others. Reading, for example, is appropriate but not confined by the school. If a child is reading, he or she may indeed be following a plan, but the plan is really determined by the child's understanding of what is read. The reading matter may be chosen by the teacher, but reading is a series of organic patterns genetically and environmentally determined by the individual. Much of the curriculum relating to reading is explaining, reviewing and discussing what has already been read. These latter teaching behaviors, in this suggested definition constitute curriculum--the actual performance of the teacher. If I am reading, I am instructing myself. I need neither a teacher nor a curriculum. If I do need instruction about reading, I learn from the behavior of the instructor.

I would like to broaden the concept of teacher to whomever serves in an instructional capacity. "Teacher" is thus anyone from whom one learns. Ivan Illich writes that "many young teen-agers, if given the proper incentives, programs and access to tools, are better than most schoolteachers at introducing their peers to the scientific exploration of plants, stars and matter, and to the discovery of how and why a motor or a radio functions" (Illich, 1970).

It seems to me appropriate, also, to define education and schooling as concepts associated with curriculum. *Education* I define as how and what people learn. *Schooling* I define as the management of selected activities for learning together with techniques for promoting it. *Curriculum* is teaching behaviors. *Instruction* is how the teacher manages teaching behaviors. The *teaching act is the curriculum.*

The postulation of a definition is not a theory, nor do I pretend it to be. But defining curriculum as teaching behaviors does place limits on investigations to follow. The chief criterion for a theory is that it is testable against information from the world. Explaining away any data without a theory because we have experienced it first-hand is not admissible in my view either, because the law governing experience may not have been understood. Witnessing falling fruit did not lead men initially to the law of gravity. To say that we have "done" curriculum is not to say that we knew what we were doing, or that we understood the laws regulating what we were doing when we were doing it.

Defining curriculum as teaching behaviors is not meant to detract from the importance of what the students do. However, there already exist several theories of how people learn, but there is little about how people teach, apart from techniques which help in the process of experimenting with a learning theory. We have in effect been testing learning theories with teaching behaviors. We have not been testing teaching behaviors with a curriculum definition based on what teachers do. Because we have been testing learning theories to determine whether or not curricula were successful, all of our experimental designs have had to include the learner who has been nearly impossible to control experimentally. And so the reasoning has been that we cannot control students' learning, so we can never validate empirically our curriculum designs.

Two further issues are essential to this proposed definition. The first is that curriculum defined as teaching behaviors must be sensitive to the requirements for *improving* teaching behaviors with increased knowledge and technical skills. The second is perhaps the most important, and that is that a curriculum definition, such as the behavior of teachers, must be joined with an appropriate learning theory in order to evaluate learning achievement.

There is a further, perhaps more fruitful area of investigation: the achievement of the teacher in the teaching act. A curriculum definition which couples itself with the teaching act allows for the development of learning while teaching. Who can say that the acceleration of one quantifiable unit of either learning achievement of technical skill development on the part of one or more teachers might not be more desirable than the quantifiable unit of learning achievement on the part of one or more students?

If curriculum is the totality of teaching behaviors, then the answer in this context is that teaching is the doing of the curriculum. Correspondingly, curriculum is the performance of teaching acts. Behaviors are characterized by their intention, even though they may appear to be random and arbitrary. Teaching behaviors intend to demonstrate the curriculum even in the broadest of interpretations. It seems important to know whether or not specific acts are intentionally teaching acts. The student does in fact learn from what is perceived from teacher behavior, despite teacher volition.

If a teacher opens a window, collects money for lunches, reprimands a child, smiles or glares at another, stares at a book--these may not normally be considered teaching actions. Yet they contain all the elements of the transmission of the culture and the personality of the teacher. They are not always part of a plan. Even if a teacher decides consciously not to teach one day at all, what students in fact learn that day, however, minimally considered in the traditional sense from the teacher, is in this context the curriculum. Indeed, how can it be otherwise?

Has any curriculum been done if, hypothetically, a student has learned nothing? According to this statement, a suggested curriculum definition is not based on whether or not students learn, crucial as that is to the schooling process. It is based on whether or not teaching behaviors occurred.

A curriculum definition does not have to include a learning theory. After all, a learning theory does not necessarily include a curriculum definition. A learning theory does not demand the presence of a teacher.

What is the test of a theory? Strong, empirical, validated data. Without precision or agreement in definition about curriculum, what can possibly constitute the empirical case for support of a curriculum theory or definitions?

Whatever we "do" to the curriculum--make it more moral, more humane, more responsive, more germane--depends on how we understand it. If, as Glenys Unruh explains, curriculum "means a plan for achieving intended learning outcomes...a plan concerned with purpose, with what is to be learned, and with the results of instruction," (Unruh, 1975) then the question must be--whose plan? If it is the plan of someone other than the teacher (even another fellow teacher) and the teacher decides not to follow the plan exactly, the theory that the curriculum is a plan crumbles because it is not testable. It therefore seems that one empirically testable theory is actual teaching performance (that *that* is the plan), whether or not it conforms to known and performed prescription. It is the demonstrated activities of the collected teachers in any given location that become meaningful to students, not necessarily the presumed plan of what should occur at any given time in any given place with any given body of knowledge.

TEACHER PLANNING AND CONTENT

Is teacher planning and preparation a part of curriculum content? Other questions which distinguish definitions have to be asked first. Is teacher planning an organizational activity whereby the teacher arranges subject content for presentation? Or is teacher planning an information quest, to acquire more knowledge about what to present? Is it a combination of both of these processes?

It may seem clear that if the teacher, as part of the planning process, is attempting to acquire new information to present, then that is a part of a learning, not a teaching, function. It may be argued that the teacher must indeed learn in order to teach. Such learning may also be preparatory to teaching, but is it essentially a part of curriculum planning? In my view, both learning more about what to teach and better organizing how to present it are necessary components in planning the teaching act, but they are preparatory to curriculum not the curriculum itself. Although the planning for the content may be logical, coherent, systematic and stimulating, it is strategically useful to the teacher but only hypothetically useful to the learner. The teacher planning function is helpful to the teacher, but its purpose is usually associated with a group, not an individualized, scheme for presentation.

To understand this curricular planning function we have only to look back at how curriculum planning was conceived and developed in the past. Recall that in the late 1950's and early 1960's the curriculum planning function was redirected from teachers to experts in fields of knowledge taught in schools. Comprehensively conceived and developed texts emerged, especially in the physical and natural sciences and mathematics, which still characterize secondary school curriculums.

Because teachers needed instruction in the new content and methods, extensive teacher training programs also emerged. It became clear, however, after extensive research investigations, that, like the language laboratories introduced for foreign language use, the mere introduction of new content was not useful unless it went hand in glove with instruction in how to use it. The profession learned that it was better in the long run to teach teachers themselves how to develop curriculum rather than to have someone plan it for them. Today, the consensus seems to be that curriculum planning has returned *pari passu* to the teachers who are more proximate to the instructional processes.

Harnischfeger and Wiley have proposed a comprehensive model, provocative in its treatment of many of the school variables, but primarily a teaching and learning model for elementary schools (Harnischfeger, 1976). The fundamental principle of the model is that what the pupil does is central to the way he or she learns, an undeniable fact often overlooked in other models. The model suggested by Harnischfeger and Wiley is an attempt to specify how students spend their time and the amounts of time they are exposed to learning.

The function of time takes on an added dimension because teachers not only present curriculum, they allocate the resources on how students will learn, in what time frames, and under what conditions. It is these conditions, according to the model, that determine pupil learning. The model has significant implications for the time teachers allot to student learning pursuits. The attractive new feature is the way in which the model relates teacher and school characteristics through the intervening variable of pupil pursuits of learning.

Student learning is, after all, what the school is all about. The purpose, therefore, of any curriculum model must ultimately be to help explain student achievement. Yet any curriculum model has to consider the role of teachers, although, as Cooley observes, research on teacher effectiveness has produced little policy change. "The major reasons for the lack of results on research on teacher effectiveness are: (a) the classroom situation has been oversimplified; (b) the relationship among pupil, teacher and curriculum has been ignored..." (Cooley, 1976).

Clearly, the Harnischfeger-Wiley model has opened new conceptual understandings in bridging empirical studies and theoretical insights. It does not, it seems to me, incorporate new information about the curriculum, apart from time spent by pupils in learning activities. Moreover, the teacher's behaviors are not as clearly defined as they might be; they are reduced largely to planning activities. Cooley notes: "There are only a few hints as to what specific teacher activities may or may not be important, and they tend to direct attention to what the teacher does out of the classroom rather than in the classroom. As everyone knows, there's many a slip between plan and execution" (Cooley, 1976).

CONCLUSION

Designing curriculum from the hypothetical point of departure of teacher behavior eliminates the hopeless debate about the "hidden" curriculum--that non-formal, out-of-school set of experiences that constitute more learning opportunities, in the minds of some, than school sometimes provides (Martin, 1976). Nothing is hidden in a framework where the sum total of teacher behavior constitutes all that the curriculum implies.

It also tends to synthesize what we understand about the nature of knowledge, (Brown, 1976) the nature of man, and the nature of society-- variables we have found impossible to experiment with meaningfully. The teaching behavior becomes the embodiment of these understandings. Thus, the nature of society is not a separate input in a curricular flow chart. It is the performance of a group of teachers in a societal setting...the school.

Curriculum is in the mind of the curriculum transmitter, and can only be learned (in an interactive sense) from the words and actions expressive of such a mind. As is true with many major theories, the one which shows the most favorable promise may be that which appears most simple and yet which has appeared most elusive. Analyzing teacher behavior may be one way for experimentors to formulate curriculum hypothesis and for the curriculum field worker to regain composure.

Chapter Two

CLASSICAL CURRICULUM TRADITIONS

THE TRADITION OF PHILOSOPHY

The methodological principle of Greek philosophy was a questioning strategy, a dialogue between two or more people. It was known as the Socratic method. As a youth Plato came under the influence of Socrates who was using the discussion method to challenge anyone who would listen how mistaken were conventional beliefs on morals. Socrates directed his listeners to something he called wisdom. The Athenian politicians had Socrates put to death on the charge of corrupting Greek youth.

In 387 B.C. Plato established his Academy in Athens and incorporated dialogue as the chief form of instruction. The instructional form determined the curricular content. According to Plato the discussants already had innate ideas and only needed articulation to become real. Dialogue was only a way of drawing out the ideas already known. Plato's *Dialogues* were a literary device using conversation and questioning between a master and pupils. Aristotle studied in Plato's Academy during Plato's last 20 years.

It was Plato who catapulted the world into modern thought. He had originally held, with Heraclitus, that all things were experiencing change and in a constant state of flux. Socrates had concluded that definitions governed the behavior of men. Plato accepted Socrates' teachings on definitions but held that a common definition was needed. Because things that were sensible, that is known through the senses, are always changing, the common definition cannot be a definition of a sensible thing. The common definition, for Plato, was Ideas. Ideas are forms of sensible things that exist elsewhere in a pure form. The forms of ideas were the causes of all things.

Plato's common definitions thus became universal ideas. Things change, decay, and die. But the idea of beauty continues and is therefore immortal. The common quality running through the essence of things constitutes the world of ideas.

A section of the dialogue from *Theaetetus* is appropriate.

"SOCRATES...I will endeavor, however, to explain what I believe to be my meaning: When you speak of cobbling, you mean the science or art of making shoes?"
"THEAETETUS...Just so."
"SOCRATES...And when you speak of carpentering, you mean the art of making wooden implements?"

"THEAETETUS...I do."
"SOCRATES...In both cases you define the subject-matter of each of the two arts."
"THEAETETUS...True."
"SOCRATES...But that, Theaetetus, was not the point of my question: we wanted to know not the subjects, nor yet the number of the arts or sciences, but we wanted to know the nature of knowledge in the abstract."

Plato's curriculum of studies was determined by the age of the pupil. From birth to 17 or 18, a pupil plays games and develops his physical abilities. After learning to read and write he is introduced to music and literature, and the elements of science. He continues meanwhile with a program of training in math, which for Plato was the essence of all science. A youth undergoes rigorous military training and physical exercise from roughly the age of 18 to 20, and then begins a program of science education in earnest. And since science is principally mathematical in form, the program of studies consists of arithmetic, geometry--plane and solid--astronomy and harmonics, a branch of music. After the age of 30, the student engages in *Dialectic* the form of dialogue by which the principle from which all knowledge flows is sought. This study in the beginning of wisdom, the search for "the idea of the good," the nature of knowledge, provides the basis for a serious understanding of the nature of the world.

As the *Dialogues* attest, philosophy was the highest curriculum study, the discussion about truths, the stretching of the mind in conversation towards a certainty that was not known before. The instructional form of a dialogue is itself a paradoxical idea in Plato's philosophy. For Plato it was the business of the search for knowledge to turn the eye of the mind (which he called "soul") from the fantasies of the world of sense and appearances to the eternal and immutable forms.

Curriculum, beginning with the origins of Western schooling, was thus a program of studies, a series of academic pursuits which culminated in whatever was understood as formal education. For nearly a 1000 years in Europe, philosophy, logic and dialectic were the crowning achievements of schooling. This tradition lasted until the last century when science and the scientific method replaced philosophy, logic and dialectic as the principal form of instruction. It is important to note here that for both Plato and Aristotle, but Aristotle particularly, that observation was also a major method of discovery.

Logic ruled throughout the Middle Ages, and was one of the primary methods of philosophy, a deductive system of argument ("argument" as a way of discovering truth, not as a heated discussion) which consists of a major and minor premise and a conclusion. A sample:

Every curriculum subject deserves praise
Geometry is a curriculum subject
Geometry deserves praise

Students who suspected geometry was not worthy of any praise, but more likely scorn and derision couldn't seem to refute the "logic" of that argument, if the major premise was accepted. It was the overuse of false arguments, the corruption of what seemed only partially true, that led the Greek sophists to use logic to convince anyone of anything. Logic was the basis for the study of rhetoric, the major subject for those training to be politicians in both Greece and Rome.

Of course the alchemists and a few geniuses like Francis Bacon, who

21

died from a cold in the 17th century after experimenting with refrigerated chickens, also used the trial and error method to gain new knowledge. But logic, as the premier methodology of philosophy and rhetoric, continued to dominate intellectual inquiry and educational thinking until recent times.

Understanding how philosophy treats first principles of all the sciences has traditionally been the foundation of an academic subject, and the basis for curriculum development. Hence, algebra, geometry, chemistry and physics begin with first principles, natural laws or theorems. Philosophy, and the traditional way of teaching, has thus been a major contributor to the organization of subject matter in schools.

Every scientist or seeker of the truth, regardless of profession or adherance to a particular theoretical bent, will have formed some kind of methodology for inquiry, a process that supposedly knows no boundaries where the quest for knowledge is concerned. The stuff of philosophy, and the related questions of truth, knowledge and beauty are today useful to the extent people find their pursuit practical and intellectually satisfying. Such questions do not always belong to one discipline or another, do not always fall neatly into a tidy academic discipline.

The disadvantage of a formal curriculum, one that is taught as if all about it were already known, is that it does not teach for what isn't known, does not build the skills necessary for re-constructing the subject. In this respect, all curriculum is history, because its intent is to teach what mankind already possesses, not what it needs to discover.

Here Dmitry Mendeleev comes to mind. Mendeleev was a Russian chemist of the last century who discovered correctly the correlation between chemical properties and their atomic weights. One day as he was about to depart Leningrad (then St. Petersburg) for an important trip, he suddenly realized that he could group certain chemical compounds. He constructed a periodic law of chemical substances by hypothesizing gaps between elements, a concept he remembered from a game of cards. He predicted, correctly as it turned out, that new elements would be discovered where gaps in the atomic weights existed. Mendeleev the theorist (some would say, philosopher) had predicted the expected properties of new elements more clearly than the chemists who later experimented with them.

Every subject, every teaching act, every curriculum, should include an emphasis on the gaps, those things not yet known about a subject. We do not want to be embarassed by the next generation in thinking, like Faust, that we know all there is to know.

It is one of the theses of this book that no systematic form of inquiry is more important than any other. All ancient and modern methods can be useful for discovering new ways to organize a set of learning activities. Therefore, philosophy as a curriculum tool is not less of an inquiry technique than, say, transcendental meditation or trial and error; nor is logic inferior to the scientific method simply because science is more contemporary. Educators who work with or in curriculum may be partial to a line of thought or school of investigation, as they might to a political party, but should not discount any legitimate quest for a better way of determining what the curriculum is.

THE LIBERAL ARTS TRADITION

The Greek philosophical tradition died out with the disintegration and collapse of the Roman Empire, when Constantine moved the capital to Constantinople, and marauding hordes from northern Europe over-ran most of Europe and sacked Rome. With Rome's cultural decline, a period of intellectual gloom settled in, and illiteracy reigned. It wasn't until the 11th century that Europe was re-introduced to Greek thought, ironically by schools of Islamic scholars.

The setting was Toledo in Spain, one of those rare hilltop cities that for centuries has been defensively fortified to withstand attack. But as early as 1085 A.D. Toledo was the site of an unusual merger in intellectual Western history: it was a multicultural urban center where Moslems, Jews and Christians mingled, and where schools of translators transcribed ancient texts from Greek (which Europe, except for a few Irish monks, had forgotten) and from Arabic and Hebrew into Latin, Europe's one remaining schooling language.

Part of this productive output was practically useful. The Islamic world had by this time perfected one of the most practical instruments of all time, the astrolabe. Astronomy--that practical science that mankind needed to fix the calendar, especially for celebrating religious feasts, in addition to regulating agriculture--was introduced into Europe by Arab texts. Greek works had been destroyed by vandals, and by such fundamentalist groups as the Christian zealots who burned the writings of Ptolemy at Alexandria in 389 A.D. While Europe lapsed into the Dark Ages, the Moslem Empire, which covered all of the southern Mediterranean from southern Spain to India to the borders of China and all of the Middle East, was collecting the written works of the Greeks, Persians and Indians and adding to that collective store of knowledge.

Muslim scholars introduced the decimal system into Europe in the 12th century A.D., after Islamic scholars had discovered it in India about 750 A.D. Algebra, almanac, zero, zenith, and scores of similar terms are Arabic in origin, and now an integral part of conventional mathematical and scientific thought and curriculum acceptance.

Thus it was that Aristotle, the realist, was "re-discovered" by Europeans and the scholastics, having been translated by Islamic scholars in Spain. The rational philosophy of Aristotle was used by Thomas Aquinas for building a compendium of Christian theology. His *Summa Theologica* became the basis of intellectual training and discussion throughout the Middle Ages, and the cornerstone of university education.

The curriculum of schools throughout the Middle Ages endured well into the middle of the last century. It is much misunderstood today. It did not consist merely of Latin and Greek. In fact, the majority of subjects were what we would consider math and science. The end of formal education, where it existed at all, was literacy, the first few years of primary training. Anything beyond that was reserved for clerics, physicians and lawyers. Thus, much of the "secondary" or university education beyond elementary schooling was philosophy, theology, medicine and law.

The curriculum of these grammar schools, which were private and not a system of state-supported education as we know it today, was the seven liberal arts, the curriculum model proposed by Aristotle. They were liberal because they were supposed to free the mind from ignorance. The curriculum was also only for free men, not slaves. The *Trivium*, the primary school, curriculum consisted of: grammar, rhetoric (spoken communication) and logic or dialectic.

The *Quadrivium*, or secondary curriculum, was: arithmetic, music, geometry, and astronomy. There was no alternative schooling curriculum, no vocational training. Apprenticing was left to the master guildsman and the guild system. Our use of the word "trivial," meaning of lesser significance, is taken from the *Trivium* because it was meant for the younger students.

The curriculum of the liberal arts remained unchanged for so long, not because it was dominated by scholastic thinking, but because all thinking, and indeed all social life, was dominated by the Church and subject to its authority. The Bible was used as the textbook for reading and spelling, and some rhetoric. There was no space for experimentation in subject content. The curriculum assumed, willy nilly, a kind of dogmatic orthodoxy.

The idea that the schooling should offer only one kind of curriculum for all students under all conditions without variability still survives in the writings of Robert Hutchins, Mortimer Adler and the tradition of the Great Books, and Harry Broudy. The discussion today, principally proposed by Adler and his associates, is not about resurrecting the liberal arts, but about standardizing the liberal arts curriculum in schools. This idea is expanded in *The Paideia Proposal* (1982). Essentially, Adler believes that there should be one course of study for all students, and that it should be applied universally the same. He repudiates the notion that there should be differentiated curricula for different students based on student needs. This traditional philosophy of the curriculum is premised on the assumption that the quest for truth is everywhere the same, and that schooling should be a common search based on the best that Western thought has to offer.

Although most curriculum workers would dismiss the uniform curriculum approach of Adler and his followers in the scholastic tradition, there are many who see merit in the Socratic approach and the emphasis on basic skills. There is a modest revival in both public and private schooling in urban America of the liberal arts tradition. The criticism is that the liberal arts curriculum tends to ignore advances in biological understanding and psychology. Nevertheless, the tradition continues in much of secondary schooling and in liberal colleges and universities. Latin may have disappeared from the curriculum, but the classical tradition is alive and well. Part of the liberal arts tradition survives in Jesuit education.

The Jesuits--The Society of Jesus--was founded in 1540 by Ignatius Loyola, a Spaniard. The first Jesuit college was founded in 1548 in Messina in Sicily. When Loyola died in 1556 there were over 300. A century later, in 1750, just a few years before the Pope suppressed the Order, the Jesuits were responsible for operating 845 educational establishments.

The Jesuit influence on schooling and the liberal arts tradition in curriculum is widespread still throughout the world. Today, worldwide, there are 817 secondary schools and 482 colleges and universities. It is a major force in private schooling. The tradition of classical studies and liberal arts from Plato and Aristotle onwards is one of its hallmark curricular features, characteristic of its curricular quality. In a sense, the Jesuits, irrespective of their missionary and religious orientation, are the last in an unbroken line of classical training programs from Plato in Greece and Quintillian in Rome. Few other groups provided formalized programs of studies for students who were preparing to govern others and assume societal leadership.

JOHN LOCKE, THE EMPIRICIST

John Locke was born in 1632 and died in 1704 having lived through a very turbulent period in English history: the beheading of Charles I, Cromwell and the Protectorate and the rule of Parliament without a monarch, to the return of monarchy and William and Mary as joint monarchs. Because of Locke's association with the Earl of Shafesbury who

THE SAME COURSE OF STUDY FOR ALL

	COLUMN ONE	**COLUMN TWO**	**COLUMN THREE**
GOALS	ACQUISITION OF ORGANIZED KNOWLEDGE	DEVELOPMENT OF INTELLECTUAL SKILLS -SKILLS OF LEARNING	ENLARGED UNDERSTANDING OF IDEAS AND VALUES
	by means of	by means of	by means of
MEANS	DIDACTIC INSTRUCTION LECTURES AND RESPONSES TEXTBOOKS AND OTHER AIDS	COACHING, EXERCISES, AND SUPERVISED PRACTICE	MAIEUTIC OR SOCRATIC QUESTIONING AND ACTIVE PARTICIPATION
	in three areas of subject matter	in the operations of	in the
AREAS OPERATIONS and ACTIVITIES	LANGUAGE, LITERATURE, AND THE FINE ARTS MATHEMATICS AND NATURAL SCIENCE HISTORY, GEOGRAPHY, AND SOCIAL STUDIES	READING, WRITING, SPEAKING, LISTENING, CALCULATING, PROBLEM-SOLVING, OBSERVING, MEASURING, ESTIMATING, EXERCISING CRITICAL JUDGMENT	DISCUSSION OF BOOKS (NOT TEXTBOOKS) AND OTHER WORKS OF ART AND INVOLVEMENT IN ARTISTIC ACTIVITIES e.g., MUSIC, DRAMA, VISUAL ARTS

THE THREE COLUMNS DO NOT CORRESPOND TO SEPARATE COURSES, NOR IS ONE KIND OF TEACHING AND LEARNING NECESSARILY CONFINED TO ANY ONE CLASS

(from THE PAIDEIA PROPOSAL Adler, 1982)

was in and out of political favor, Locke had to spend several years of his life in exile in Holland. But while in Holland, he became acquainted withWilliam and Mary, and when they came collectively to power he returned to England for the greatest period of his productive life.

"The differences to be found in the manners and abilities of men is owing more to their education than to anything else," said Locke in his *Some Thoughts Concerning Education.* England in the 17th century had no formal system of schooling, although there were schools for boys and schools for girls. But there was no supervision of education, no state-sponsored schooling.

Locke's principal work on schooling, which contains a major analysis of curriculum as a proposed program of studies, was not meant for educators, but was intended as a guide for the tutoring of sons of the leisure class. It was a series of essays written to an aristocratic friend. The curriculum in the schools of Locke's day was desperately narrow in scope, and in fact, Locke was not interested in schools at all. But he was interested in education and in schooling for the elite.

What was common sense about schooling 300 years ago does not have the advantages of modern research and scholarship. For example, Locke thought of learning as a passive, a receptive not an active process. His metaphor of a young mind as a *tabula rasa,* a clean or blank slate, might sound anathema to geneticists and developmental psychologists. His description of the mind of a student is as "white paper or wax to be moulded."

Locke's appeal is his ability to crystalize thinking about the content of education. He established a trend later to influence American scholars, particularly Thomas Jefferson who developed a similar course of studies which did help shape both the function and form of American constitutional and representative government.

Locke minimized his own writings on curriculum and education, but his vigorous and lively prose style made what he had to say captivating to his readers. He had been a lecturer and tutor at Oxford after receiving his M.A. degree there in 1658. He taught Greek and Rhetoric. He was a qualified physician, but never practiced that profession except for friends. He wrote on a variety of topics: politics, philosophy, theology and education. His education writings are based on actual teaching experiences and tutorial responsibilities, and on his guardianship of a few children of noble families entrusted to his care throughout his life. He was a frequent private tutor. He never married and never had children of his own.

Locke was one of those pioneeers, like Descartes and Bacon, who revitalized the Aristoteleian method of scientific inquiry, of an empirical approach to acquiring knowledge. He acknowledged that learning takes place best when acquired through the senses, not through abstract reasoning. Locke, and his Scottish philosopher contemporary David Hume, planted the seeds which would later develop into modern experimental psychology, cognitive processing and theories of learning.

Locke's *Essay Concerning Human Understanding* lays the framework for his overall concept of how the mind functions. This classical work forms the basis for the inductive and empirical method which transformed philosophical thinking about how children learn and the mind works. It is still fundamental to cognitive psychologists and theorists. Only research into brain studies and medicine and anatomy have updated our understanding of brain functioning and activities we call thinking.

Locke influenced also later education specialists like Pestalozzi and Froebel. Locke's stature and influence was unrivaled in England for at least 150 years until John Stuart Mill who pointedly acknowledged his debt to Locke in his own thinking.

century before substantive changes were made in the curriculum. When schools did change their curricular programs, many approximated Locke's proposals.

Reading
Writing
English Composition (spoken...like rhetoric)
Languages (Latin,Greek, French)
Grammar (only after knowledge of a language)
Science (natural philosophy)
Other Subjects (arithmetic, geography, history)
Practical Activities (travel, riding, wrestling,
　　　learning a trade, leisure interests)

In some ways this program of studies looks surprisingly contemporary. Locke's curriculum proposals were a transition from the best of the classical tradition to the practicality of the contemporary curricula. There is a hint of this in the category Locke calls "practical activities," where he includes much of what we would call physical education. But the part about "learning a trade" we would now classify as vocational or career education. And "leisure interests," I believe, opens wide the door to curricular aspects focused on student areas of interest and on livelong learning pursuits.

Locke's own personal interests were as broad as those he outlined. He had what is still now considered to be one of the oldest surviving collections of English wild flowers. He collected over 3000 different species in two volumes. Many still retain their original color. He had a personal library of 3,675 volumes, a considerable scholarly investment in any era.

His innovative education thinking extended beyond the curriculum. He jettisoned the idea of age-readiness, as if all children should begin school at age seven, and proposed that children should begin reading as soon as they can talk. In this he challenged all established traditional schooling practice. He believed in play in learning, never a popular idea among schoolmen. His preference was for students to make credible progress in learning, even at the expense of systematic compulsion; to let marked achievement suffer a little rather than allow discontent for studies to set in. He again departed from tradition when he suggested that grammar, the mainstay of primary schooling throughout the centuries, should only be studied by mature students. He did not consider grammar as important for a study of ordinary discourse or for the child's understanding of language and its uses. Grammar should only be studied when a student knows a language.

Like a true Renaissance intellectual, Locke emphasized the primacy of intellect and reason in the formation of character against, for example, the crudities of corporal punishment for the young, a typical practice of schooling. He proposed that truth is an end in itself--very Platonic--an inevitable example of his incubation in the scholastic tradition. With some minor inconsistencies, he was utilitarian, anticipating J.S. Mill and the pragmatism, of the American Henry James. He was a budding pragmatist in matters relating to children's education, their upbringing and intellectual development. He made sense to his readers. He renounced Plato and rejected the conventional belief in innate ideas. He believed instead that ideas come from sense experiences, a radical concept in his day. He was thus a pioneer in advocating that to learn we must first experience. As a philosopher, I believe he gave birth to curricular empiricism.

JEAN JACQUES ROUSSEAU, THE ROMANTICIST

> Education comes to us from nature, from
> man, and from things. The inner growth
> of our organs and faculties is the
> education of nature, the use we make of
> this growth is the education of men, what
> we gain by our experience of our sur-
> roundings is the education of
> things.
>
> Rousseau, *Emile*

Jean Jacques Rousseau (1712-1778) was one of the first theorists of individualism, and his writings signaled a distinct change in philosophy and educational thought. He didn't think much of institutions, including schools, because he thought of them as corrupting influences. In his view institutions inhibited individual freedom and liberty. This was an outrageous idea at the time, and flew in the face of the Church, the monarchy, and every established social organization. But his influence gave impetus to the French Revolution only a decade after his death.

Rousseau believed that the child was born good. This ran contrary to the Church's doctrine of original sin. He was labeled the first romantic because of his beliefs that the best education for the young was to escape from the suffocating influence of society. He said that children should learn away from schools in the freedom of nature.

I have included a brief analysis of Rousseau here, not because he offered any specific prescriptions for curriculum or schooling, but because his educational philosophy profoundly revolutionized subsequent schooling practices. He can perhaps be considered as the first of the advocates of the deschooling movement.

Perhaps his philosophy can best be summarized in his own words:

> I am never weary of repeating: let all the lessons
> of young people take the form of doing rather than
> talking; let them learn nothing from books which they
> can learn from experience.

He said that if a child was to learn astronomy that he should go watch sunsets, and observe the motion of the stars. If a child were to learn geography, he learns it best by beginning with his house, then his neighborhood, and his environs. Comenius had suggested his same approach in the previous century.

Rousseau began his major education work, *Emile*, at the request of a woman interested in the education of her son. *Emile* was intended as a short essay but grew into a major book. He lobbied for the study of children as children, not for what they might become as adults. And anyone who examines the portrait paintings of the early 18th century will observe how artists depicted children as small adults, with their small, round faces clothed in adult garb gazing out bewilderedly into a grown-up world.

If we consider curriculum as a category of schooling, Rousseau offers us nothing. But if we think of curriculum as experiences that aid development, Rousseau is the first major proponent who suggests that experiences are the stuff of schooling not something extra.

He rejected the prevailing belief that knowlege alone constitutes the structure of what we know. Until Descartes in the century before Rousseau, the concept of intellect, in the tradition of the scholastics and rational philosophers, reigned supreme and unchallenged. Because the rationalist philosophy was extensively developed by Thomas Aquinas, and incorporated Plato and Aristotle, it was approved by the Church, which controlled all public policy. Rousseau's doctrine was a challenge to the faith and so he was out of favor, on the proscribed list of books, and therefore his popularity rose with the masses.

One of his major contributions to Western thought was that knowledge alone was not a necessity for an education. His emphasis on nature found a devoted following in England, and in the poetry of Wordsworth, Keats, Shelley and Byron. Thus, indirectly Rousseau has had a major impact on the curriculum of modern schools in English literature.

Rousseau's thinking began a radical departure in philosophy and education. His intellectual followers had to look elsewhere than rational philosophy for assumptions upon which to base the structure of institutions, including schools, the nature of knowledge, and the content of the curriculum. The concept of the individual, not the concept of knowledge, was the new key. John Dewey is the logical intellectual disciple of Rousseau. Dewey's ideas about the curriculum developed because of his belief that the child precedes curricular content. The child, not the structure of knowledge or the nature of the curriculum, would compel consideration. Educators like Pestalozzi, Froebel and Maria Montessori would, following Rousseau, place the child central to curriculum planning and not just peripheral to it. Within Rousseau are the theoretical beginnings of the Progressive Education movement in the U.S. from the 1920's to the 1960's.

HERBERT SPENCER, THE UTILITARIAN

> To suppose that deciding whether a math-
> ematical or a classical education is the best, is
> deciding what is the proper curriculum, is much
> the same thing as to suppose that the whole of
> dietetics lies in ascertaining whether or not bread
> is more nutritive than potatoes.
> Spencer, *Education*

Two significant books were published within two years of each other in England in the middle of the last century: in 1859 Darwin published *Origin Of The Species*, and in 1861 Herbert Spencer came out with *Education: Intellectual, Moral and Physical*. Darwin's book, of course, polarized the community of his day--as it does schooling practice in many communities at the present--by repudiating the historical accuracy of the Bible regarding man's origin, by intimating mankind's animal origins, and by emphasizing biological as opposed to spiritual development. Darwin's concept of evolution has continued to spawn new theoretical and empirical research investigations.

Spencer's *Education* also had a major impact on curriculum thinking because Spencer argued forcefully for the inclusion of science in the school's curriculum. Spencer believed that science was more useful than language in preparing the young for what he called a "complete living." In the opening chapter of *Education* entitled "Of What Knowledge is Most Worth," Spencer lists a taxonomy of the kinds of learning that characterizes life. In order of importance, they are:

> self-preservation
> the necessaries of life
> the rearing and discipline offspring
> the maintenance of proper social and
> political relations
> skills for the leisure part of life

He divided knowledge into its value to mankind. The value was either intrinsic, quasi-intrinsic or conventional. He concluded that knowledge which was of intrinsic value should take precedence over other values. And what knowledge was that, he asked? His answer was science. For Spencer, school and curriculum needs had to be related to life. The curriculum should not have an existence monastically separate from the real world. Educators still argue that schools have curricula that are too removed from practical life problems. Others argue that schools often model too closely life's concerns, especially vocational education, and don't develop the mind enough. The prevailing view is that curriculum decisions are the result of value choices within a community.

Spencer anticipated, in his concept of self-preservation curricula which have found favor today: the value of good nutrition, of keeping a healthy body, of proper diet and exercise, of maintaining the life of the organism. This is more than a component of elementary or secondary education, or of health and physical education. It is a matter of curriculum content following appropriate life priorities. Spencer may be the first to suggest that what should be included in programs of study are experiences which lead to a more productive and happy life. He departs from offering a syllabus of course offerings and proposes instead dimensions that the curriculum should include.

By arguing for the larger, more relevant, category of preserving and maintaining a more rewarding life, Spencer has in a sense elevated the curriculum from a course of studies outline to the idea of the value of personal rewards obtained from schooling. He has gone beyond schooling just for the benefit of the intellectual life. It is a compelling idea, and has substantively influenced curriculum development in this generation.

Here is some of what he says:

> To prepare us for complete living is the
> function which education has to discharge; and
> the only rational mode of judging an educational
> course is to judge in what degree it discharges
> such function.

To paraphrase: education, and by implication the curriculum or course of studies, fails if it does not prepare students for life skills.

Spencer was also an advocate for mental evolution. Locke had also been a proponent of the maturation of the intellect, but Locke's focus was on the nurture side, on the role of sense experiences and the environment. Spencer, however, incorporated Darwin's new thinking about the mind evolving as an organism. Thus, Spencer's prescription is for the developmental process to mature. "...A higher morality, like a higher intelligence, must be reached by slow growth." And in another place he says: "...so in education we are finding that success is to be achieved only by making our measures subservient to that spontaneous unfolding which all minds go through in their progress towards maturity." It is an idea that is reminiscent of Plato, this unfolding of the mind, and yet, because of its timing, seems surprisingly contemporary because it comes alongside of Darwin's hypotheses. Are the teaching act, and the curriculum, to be merely aids to mental evolution? Or is the curriculum's intent to be as the provider for experiences that lead to intellectual maturity? Is the priority on natural evolution or on environmental determinants? These questions still puzzle and entertain educators.

His prose is still elegant and in the best tradition of rhetorical argumentation. Spencer was a product of the classical tradition but responsive to the key ideas of his day. His discussion of moral education was mainly on behalf of the upbringing of children by parents, a fulmination against ill-prepared parents in raising children. Skills in parenting were central to his curriculum for schools.

He sided more with Darwin than with Rousseau in the place of the child in the curriculum. He says: "During early years every civilized man passes through that phase of character exhibited by the barbarous race from which it is descended...The popular idea that children are 'innocent,' while it is true with respect to evil knowledge, is totally false with respect to evil impulses, as half an hour's observation in the nursery will prove to anyone." Clearly, Rousseau was not in Spencer's favor. But the notion that children descend in an evolutionary sense was unmistakenly Darwinian.

Chapter Three
CONTEMPORARY CURRICULUM CONCEPTS

CONTEMPORARY PERSPECTIVES OF CURRICULUM

The word *theory* often conjures terror, fright, and avoidance behavior among many teachers. Why is it that a new perspective for obtaining knowledge should be so ridiculed by society's dispensers of traditional knowledge? The root meaning is uncomplicated enough. A theory is the "act of viewing." It once meant an imaginative contemplation of reality, like poetry. In education, its more common meaning is a principle or a plan of action.

A theory is also a causal system, an attempt to construct a framework for understanding natural forces. Each theory is given additional credibility by accumulated evidence which appears to confirm the theory's explanation of how a phenomenon occurs. However, over time, many theories fail to explain some unusual occurrence, recently discovered, and the search is on for a new set of guidelines, a new hypothesis, upon which to confirm or deny similar occurrences. A theory is mankind's perpetual striving for rules which predict or explain events.

Theories of human behavior tend to follow the same pattern as theories of natural science. But they are somewhat different in that theories of human behavior try to encompass organic development and the full range of human behavior under all conditions. Educational theories attempt to describe and explain human behavior as it influences the process of education in schools.

The contemporary education theories, partly rooted in psychology, focus on "stages" of human development, like Piaget's stages of mental development, Erikson's stages of affective growth, and Kohlberg's stages of moral development. No one theory seems to offer a complete explanation for human development in all its multifaceted dimensions.

A theory does not begin from nothing. It builds on tradition. But all theories are born of the first principle of scientific investigation-- observation. Theories about human behavior are less resistant to change because people seem to resist falling under someone's theory when they act the way they do. Similarly, theories about education, about knowledge, about curriculum are distrusted even more because the research evidence is often contradictory and unconvincing. Sometimes the study of a theory in education appears to be a detached exercise for educators.

In the final analysis, theories of education and curriculum have likely been unimaginatively taught and probably imperfectly applied. Moreover, theories of curriculum do not evoke passionate interest or intellectual excitement, nor do they seem to demonstrate much relevance to classroom instruction. This is partly because so few educators--George Beauchamp and the neo-Marxists are some of the exceptions--have articulated the arena of concern and the critical issues. But Beauchamp's conclusion in 1961 in his book *Curriculum Theory* was that curriculum theory was non-existant, and his concluding remarks were a challenge to develop models and procedures for erecting a theory.

Theories or models of the curriculum, moreover, have suffered from over-simplification. Many of these conceptions of the curriculum have been reduced to popularization, and are descriptions of either what schooling is about, or what the curriculum should be accomplishing. The contemporary conceptions of the curriculum are frequently reduced to three: the knowledge-centered, the child-centered, and society-centered.

KNOWLEDGE AS CURRICULUM: ORGANIZING THE CURRICULUM

> ...philosophy may even be defined as the
> general theory of education.
> John Dewey, *Democracy And Education*

Unquestionably, schools are in the knowledge business, transmitting the distillations of the past to the young. Proponents of the knowledge-based curriculum, like Hirst and Phenix, believe that the mind is the most important faculty. According to the traditional view, espoused by those in the tradition of the liberal arts, the essence of the curriculum should consist of what has always been taught in schooling, like the structure of grammar and Euclid's theorems. The argument is that these subjects are timeless, true, always will be true, and form the backbone of educated thought.

On the other hand, some curriculum writers believe that new knowledge can be generated through discovery techniques, or inquiry approaches. The idea is a popular one, but strangely un-practiced, supposedly because it presumes uncertainty, and there is risk and some anxiety in not knowing what is expected. The ultimate goals should never be in question, and many avenues should be provided for achieving terminal objectives. That is the accepted posture. But in practice, discovery, as a demonstrated technique for learning, is observed more in the omission.

So then is knowledge impersonal and abstract, something once known by great minds, but now confined to chillingly dull texts? Or is the encounter with the great ideas of the known past a unique reconstruction of the world, a personal experience, that helps in putting into perspective contemporary concerns? The world will be different for today's students than it was for yesterday's. Will the general education background equip them for living in that information technology environment? The pertinent question is: Is yesterday's curriculum sufficient preparation for tomorrow's realities? Will the liberal arts, as we know them, be as relevant in the future as they have been in the past, or should we be designing a new liberal arts formula?

What passes for general education requirements in secondary schools is a pale reminder of what were the liberal arts. Philosophy, the faded queen of the sciences, is no longer taught. Few teachers have even had a philosophy course in their training. Math is taught as if there have been no developments since Pythagoras, and geometry as if nothing was new since Euclid. Knowledge, like the whole of the curriculum, is indeed tentative. But the knowledge-based curriculum of secondary schools follows no conceptual rationale except the teaching of the traditional academic subjects: math, science, English, social studies (a sort of poor man's excursion through history), physical education, and perhaps a foreign language. There are always more electives than requirements.

The trend in modern sciences is towards interdisciplinary studies, towards areas of problem solving that merge fields of inquiry. Biochemistry as a field was unheard of until recently. It is the emerging knowledge fields--information technology, computer sciences, systems analysis, genetic engineering, to name a few--that will shape how educated people conceive of the world in the future.

In the early 1960's Jerome Bruner in *The Process of Education* proposed that curriculum be developed based on the structure of academic disciplines. Subsequently, major national curricula--for biology, chemistry, physics and math--were developed by experts in the U.S. By the mid-1970's, based on the results of the nationally developed curricula, Bruner revised his thinking to include feedback based on students and teachers. The curricula developed by leading academicians were well organized, but not always suitable for certain groups of students. Moreover, teachers had not been consulted in this massive project, and were understandably miffed. Teachers, who had never behaved as a scientist or investigator, had trouble leading students to discovery. The structure of the discipline as perceived by the scientist did not fit well into the structure of general education.

In 1964 Philip Phenix's *Realms Of Meaning* offered a logical formula for the general education curriculum. Phenix argued that the highest good of education was to help the individual realize all the distinctly human capabilities, and that this consisted mainly in a life of meaning. Meaning was to be shaped by fulfillment in "mastery," "belonging to a community", "many-sidedness," "integrity," and "quality of understanding." The general education curriculum provides these meanings through *Symbolics* (language and math); *Empirics* (the sciences); *Ethics* and *Synoptics* (the social sciences, including history, religion and philosophy).

Teachers in secondary schools have traditionally been hired as subject matter specialists, and consequently hiring practices have perpetuated the continued dominance of the academic subject curriculum.

Perhaps what the general education curriculum needs most is a new synthesis of the major concepts that shape the world of knowledge and science, not just a new taxonomy for existing subjects. Ideas like the origin of man and the universe will always engage our best thinking, and have never been idle questions to be solved only by philosophers, theologians and astrophysicists. The concept of force involves a partial knowledge of physics but perhaps also psychology. The biological process of development now has well established theories and a research base, but there is so much unknown.

The general education program proposed in many reform statements for undergraduates in higher education follows a similar pattern of development, but could serve as a model for a new conception of general education for secondary schools. The "subjects" are: Language, Art, Heritage, The Social Web, Nature, Work, Identity. These global and multi-dimensional themes permit both amplification and contraction of curriculum units, and help both the curriculum planner and student better perceive relationships.

Judson, in *The Search For Solutions*, proposes nine central concepts that propel modern thinking, not just in science. These are: investigation, pattern, change, chance, feedback, modeling, predictions, evidence, theory. Similarly, these themes could form the basis for a general education core.

Lord Kelvin at the turn of the century is reported to have announced that physics was a finished science, needing only tidying up in a few areas. What he didn't foresee was quantum physics, Xrays, and relativity. Suddenly, the whole discipline of physics was up for grabs, and had to begin an investigation of its central purposes again. Most sciences are at that point: of re-arranging their "proven" premises, and starting from an un-tested viewpoint. General education, as a premise, should begin with the notion that what is known today will likely be discarded tomorrow, because that is the hard lesson of human knowledge...that we aren't even close to having it right at all. We must teach the young that what is generally accepted as true now will quite possibly be laughable in a few years. i wasn't taught about quarks, those microscopic particles, when I went to school; but does anyone really know what they are now, even though we've named them?

The most perplexing mysteries to me now are biological: how we got started; how we keep going; how our brain works; how we end. What I am trying to convey is a consolidation of our human quest for new knowledge and imparting that to the next generation. What I sense is happening is not that, but a weak residue of known facts, a compendium of what is taken for granted, and not an overall sense that nothing is absolute. The engaging intellectual questions of our time appear to be those that have always mystified philosophers and scientists: the origin of the universe; the origin of life; the evolution of the person; the influence of the forces in nature.

Strict adherence to the discipline doctrine of curriculum development came into question even by its staunchest advocates in the U.S. during the student protests of the war in Vietnam. Political activity galvanized social consciousness. The formal schooling curriculum had no fall-back position, no curriculum for coping with student affective processes. The curriculum had no corresponding line of inquiry into social dilemmas, personal or moral problems, as it did for structured domains of knowledge. Even Phenix's concept of personal meanings consisted of the structure of history, religion and philosophy--hardly the intellectual stuff necessary for a young man considering to be a conscientious objector in a time of war for his country, and a time of personal agony for himself. It isn't that the systematic inquiry of philosophy or religion can't help develop intellectual ability, but that the disciplines allowed for little variation based on student level of development.

In fact, a few of the major proponents of academic curriculum, such as Schwab, Phenix and Bruner, later in their careers argued for more social relevance in the curriculum. As a result, the literature on the academic disciplines ran cold, and a new wave of curriculum reform began calls for more attention to the personal needs of students. What has come to be known as a wave of so-called permissiveness began, until it too, as a movement, declined as quickly as did the national test scores. A call for "back to basics" re-emphasized rudimentary skills.

THE STUDENT AS CURRICULUM

> Anything which can be called a study, whether
> arithmetic, history, geography, or one of the nat-
> ural sciences, must be derived from materials
> which at the outset fall within the scope of
> ordinary life experience.
> John Dewey, *Experience And Education*

The contemporary child-centered approach to the curriculum originally rose in the early part of the 20th century because of the inhumane treatment of children, from the extremes described by Dickens in his novels, to the passage of child labor laws restricting working hours for children. Its most devoted and illustrious exponent was John Dewey who proposed that the curriculum be built on life experiences.

In fact, Dewey believed that a person's interest was synonymous with the concept of self. He says in *Democracy And Education:* "In fact, self and interest are two names for the same fact; the kind and amount of interest actively taken in a thing reveals and measures the quality of selfhood which exists."

A monograph entitled *The Care of Destitute, Neglected and Delinquent Children,* published in New York in 1900 by Homer Folks, caused a social stir. It caught the attention of the President of the U.S., and Theodore Roosevelt used the controversy generated to open the first White House Conference on Education in 1909. Homer Folks played a key role in the next four White House conferences on education, but his monograph, I believe, was the turning point for the nation's focus on the plight of children, and the necessity for their schooling.

The notion that schooling for children is a social imperative is a relatively recent phenomenon, and a somewhat romantic one. Rural life in America in the first 350 years of its history was not dominated by the school, but by the farm and the church. The cycles of sun and weather took precedence over schooling; school buildings were only populated during the winter months. Children were needed during the planting and harvesting season, and book learning occured only when farm life was slack. Jamestown didn't have a school for the first hundred years of its existence.

Emphasis on the child centered approach does not allow teachers or curriculum planners to neglect student interest. On the other hand, few educators believe that an entire curriculum program can be developed around student interest, although the alternative school movement points to both the strengths and weaknesses of such attempts.

Advances in learning theory, in research on achievement, and relations between the home and schooling environments clearly point to individual differences independent of traditional beliefs about the curriculum. Recent evidence in brain studies has broadened the base of understanding about how people think. The child-centered theory of curriculum stresses the belief that learning occurs best under conditions the learner values.

Children's interests, however, may not be an adequate index of their developmental needs. For example, lack of interest may reflect an imperfect curriculum, or lack of readiness skills prior to the learning experience and not just a maturational deficiency. As McNeil says, there should be no "tyranny of fixed age level norms." Large individual variations in learning are possible under variable learning conditions. A uniform curriculum, offered to all equally, may not immediately reveal these truly individual differences.

Developmental psychologists believe that the curriculum, however defined, should approximately parallel the developing mental processes of the student. According to the developmentalists, the teacher should see to it that each teaching activity matches the ability level of the intended students. Assuming, then, that students will be operating at varying levels nearly always, the curriculum should have enough flexibility to allow for different stages of growth towards the established criteria.

There are at present no recognized measuring strategies for discerning when any individual student is at a particular learning stage. The domain still falls within teacher intuition or best guess. The relationship between theories of learning, stages of cognitive growth, the curriculum and teaching practices, is very ambiguous indeed. The next area of applied research is to base a set of teaching and learning activities on stages of mental growth.

SOCIETY AS CURRICULUM

Find books with "society" in the title and usually the discussion within is on social class, cultural subgroups, ethnic or schooling achievement differences, but not specifically about society as a concept. The root meaning comes from the Latin *socius*--a companion and this is still the first meaning. But the other common meaning is a group of people sharing common interests, a community. Thus, from a sociological point of view, the community, not the child or the tradition, determines the foundation of the curriculum.

The most central questions to be considered in this approach concern the boundaries of the community. Is the society limited to the neighborhood school? The county? The political unit? The nation? The culture? The continent? The world? In point of fact, all curricula are circumscribed by national or political boundaries and hence determined by the national emphasis. Educators may believe that they are apolitical, but the multiple intersections of schooling and politics belie that assumption. Schools, and by implication the curriculum, may be un- connected with political parties, but they are nonetheless agents of government which administer the curriculum to youth who are compelled by law to attend. Except for the neo-Marxists and Wirt and Kirst, there has been little analysis of the political perspective in curriculum research.

Thus, in one sense, to pose the question, does society determine the nature of the curriculum, is irrelevant, because the nature of the political bonding means that the state controls the curriculum of those schools in the public domain.

There are, of course, nongovernmental agencies whose collective power sometimes exceeds even national government. In the U.S., the power of national and regional accrediting agencies and testing organizations, like Educational Testing Service, exerts tremendous leverage on schools to maintain standards and develop uniform curriculum procedures. In the U.S., unlike other industrialized nations, there is no national curriculum. But the private, national testing agencies create an influence on curriculum that functions in much the same way as a nationally mandated curriculum. The desire for local schools, parents and students, to take part in nationally administered tests demonstrates the power of the testing agencies' control over curricular decisions.

The compulsion for standardization is also a principal reason why schools choose published texts, and rarely allow teachers to write their own materials. Consequently, the publishers of school books have a disproportionately powerful effect on curriculum. On the other hand, publishers will not try to outwit a community and slip into text units that are controversial.

Should schools exist to train people to change the nature of society, as the Social Reconstructionists and Marxists suggest? Should the nature of the technological society (really the economic basis) determine the nature of the curriculum? Based on the idealized state, should schools as we know them exist at all, as Ivan Illich and Paulo Freire have postulated? How relevant is even general education when so much of the world is illiterate?

One method for deciding the extent of society's influence on curriculum is to compare differing societal approaches to the same phenomena. The

American Revolution may stand as an example. What might be the differences in two standard school texts on this topic in British schools and in American schools? Such differences, translated into objectives, content, attitudes and learning activities, will reflect the societal differences on the same topic and, by implication, the influence of society on the curriculum.

Plato believed that education should create in children a kind of government which would allow them to enter society. He says that the guardians of the state (they are of course the philosophers) establish their rule through education. In Book IX of *The Republic* he says:

> We should not allow them to be free until we
> establish a government within them, as we did
> in the city, fostering the best in them with what
> is best in ourselves and securing within the
> child a similar guardian and ruler, and then let
> him go free.

Thus, for Plato, entrance into society as a free person means enduring education which purges unhealthy instincts by creating a rule of interior law. Children have to have their souls ordered to be permitted to be free in the state or society. Plato didn't have much faith in the character and ability of most humans, as they could not live their own lives. They had to be guided by the philosopher rulers. Society was not democratic.

One view of the curriculum is challenged by a new wave of social reconstructionists. As Henry Giroux states: "The foundation for a new mode of curriculum must be as deeply historical as it is critical...as an extension of historical consciousness." For many of these curriculum critics, the value of the curriculum is a form of "cultural capital," and needs to be "emancipated." The purpose of "emancipation" is to free the individual ultimately from the conditions that bind them to exploitation and oppression. This approach stems historically from the German philosophers Hegel and Fichte, and thence from Marx and Engels and contemporary neo-Marxist exponents. History, and the so-called predetermined cycles that govern it (Hegel's thesis-antithesis-synthesis view of history), is the focal point of the proper study of society and the curriculum according to this view, and the politics and economics of class struggles.

Neo-Marxist political thought views schooling as exerting a hegemony over the consciousness of individuals that completely saturates and dominates their social experience. Thus, the curriculum is a form of cultural hegemony, not merely a manipulation of the individual. Neo-Marxist economic thought is ruled by analyses that show the unequal processes in schooling, in the division of labor, mobility, the processes of selection, and other economic determinants created by the school. Such analyses of the curriculum reveal, according to this line of thinking, "competing conceptions of social and ecomomic power and ideologies," as Michael Apple says.

Dwayne Huebner makes a fascinating comparison between Marx and Piaget both of whom, he says, ground their theories in human activity, Marx focusing on labor and Piaget on biological development. Marx characterized labor as alienated productive activity because man did not receive the full benefits of capital for his labors. Marx developed the concept of human activity through the social dimension--labor, production, capital, commodities, and similar concepts. Piaget, on the other hand, emphasizes the operations that both determine and condition human activity.

To the extent that the child becomes alienated, walled off, from the adult world, the child's isolated activity is a distortion of the social reality. The life of the child needs to be measured, not against the curriculum, but against adult life.

Franklin Bobbitt, in his classic study *The Curriculum* published in 1918, may appear a bit quaint when he discusses the nature of a good citizen and the development of civic consciousness. But he deplored the creation of a nation-state which raised anti-social behavior to the level of patriotism, and decorated with honor those who killed in the name of duty. Europe and America had just completed World War I and received an introduction into the horrors of modern, mechanized warfare. Nevertheless, he espoused "learning through living," and for him that included teaching students to relive wars so they could learn about conflicts. Bobbitt saw this kind of curricular experience as a way of teaching youth how life contends with opposing forces.

Although Bobbitt's curriculum foundation leans towards student interest, his focus is large: "human nature and human affairs" is his point of departure. Bobbitt saw civic training as experience in a large group, and civic consciousness as involving the student in the life of the community, the nation, even the world. On the subject of societal consciousness, Bobbitt has 45 pages. As a contrast, he has only 6 pages on moral and religious education.

There are advocates who maintain that the proper study of society and its role in schooling is in the future, and critics who hold that society doesn't have much future unless it concerns itself with the biosphere and the immediate problems of over-population, despoliation, environmental waste, and--the ultimate concern--the possibility of total nuclear annihilation. The arguments here are that the young (and hence the curriculum by implication) cannot be ignorant of what the future of the race and the planet portends. It is an argument for the possible future, not just the past, in the curriculum.

Tradition, the child, the society--should one predominate over the other, or should there be a proper balance? A healthy mix of curricular conceptions is preferable to excessive intake of only one.

Chapter Four

CURRICULUM AS CRAFT

> The great thing to be minded in education
> is, what habits you settle; and therefore in
> this, as in all other things, do not begin to
> make any thing customary.
> John Locke, *Some Thoughts Concerning Education*

The phrase "curriculum as craft" seems to hint that the planning of the academics of schooling could proceed from a vocational emphasis. But contemporary curriculum emphasis, with its focus on defined and clear objectives, historically has come from industrial and technological models of efficiency. A craft is a skill in planning and doing, and a craftsman is an artisan who has created an artifact with skill and possibly dexterity. I use the word in the same sense as statecraft. Curriculumcraft is the art of conducting curriculum affairs. Curriculum objectives have held a paramount place in schooling, and it is this functional influence on the curriculum that I want to discuss in this chapter.

OBJECTIVES AS CURRICULUM

Ralph Tyler's seminal work *Basic Principles of Curriculum And Instruction* was not published until 1949 although he had evolved the model in the 1930's while evaluating the Eight Year Study, one of the first major assessments of schooling. Tyler identified four major questions for development:

> What educational purposes should the school seek to attain?
> What educational experiences can be provided that are likely
> to attain these purposes?
> How can these educational experiences be effectively organized?
> How can we determine whether these purposes are being
> attained?

These questions are a logical procedure, from a schooling perspective, of the development of a curriculum program. They do not specify the basis of a curriculum departure. They assume that the institution of the school has the obligation to construct its best operational procedures. However, the logical sequence could just as easily be used for any other curriculum departure. For example, if we take the first question, we can substitute "school" for "student," "society," "subject," "nation" and the developmental

40

steps would still be coherent. The influences on the curriculum are not subordinated, but the curriculum developer must choose judiciously which are appropriate.

The Eight Year Study (1933-41), for which Tyler was the research director, had proposed a nearly identical formula for curriculum development: 1) the identification of objectives; 2) the selection of means for attaining objectives; 3) the organization of these means; and 4) the evaluation of the outcomes. This same sequence closely resembles Dewey's essentials for inquiry or reflection in his book *How We Think*. Thus, even by the time of Tyler's formulation there existed a clear transition between the development of objectives and the provision of learning experiences based on objectives.

Tyler commented, over a quarter century after the publication of *Basic Principles of Curriculum And Instruction*, that he would not alter the structure of the procedures but would give greater emphasis to the active role of the student in the learning process, and to the non-school areas of learning. He stressed that curriculum objectives should be selected for their importance to the learner and be capable of meaning and interest to students.

Tyler's curriculum development model, now known as a "rational" model, places the process of curriculum in the hands of the school. But clearly, various forces will align with the student, the societal aims, and the organized subject matter. There is a danger, as even Dewey warned, in treating these elements separately and ignoring their inter-dependence and relatedness. Each can become the basis for a curriculum, but not totally nor in isolation from the influences of the learner, society, and subject disciplines.

Focusing attention too insistently on the needs of the student in curriculum development can tend to ignore the elements of societal change, such as the student protest movements against war and political crisis in government in the U.S. in the late 1960's and early 1970's. Similarly, ignoring the shifting developmental needs, both biological and psychological, of children and youth in favor of current and fashionable social and political events can damage curriculum perspective.

The 1953 publication of the yearbook of the National Society for the Study of Education was entitled *Adapting The Secondary School Program To The Needs Of Youth*. But the volume never came to grips with student needs which always got translated into society needs, and the preparation of youth for adult entrance into that society. Witness the following quotation, which defined student needs as the subjects students should take.

> By and large needs, in the sense that the term is
> used generally, refer to the knowledge, habits,
> and skills which all citizens should possess in
> order to function effectively as adult citizens in
> our society. These learning products are expected
> to be mastered through the study of systematically
> organized subjects or fields of knowledge. Since
> the vast majority of secondary schools rely upon
> an officially adopted set of textbooks for the basic
> materials of instruction, the so-called common
> needs are met largely by means of "lessons"
> assigned from the textbooks.

It would seem that students do not really have needs apart from the lesson plans already organized for them. It is an unbelievable argument that justifies the existing curriculum of the school, ignores student interests and special aptitudes, and concedes that individual differences can be overcome with requirements. Yet ludicrous as it may appear, taking courses is exactly what school is all about. The systematized conveyor belt subject matter mentality is precisely the way most secondary schools propose the curriculum.

Hilda Taba's sequence for curriculum development (*Curriculum Development*, 1962) takes student needs into account, and in her seven step procedure prescribes a diagnosis of student needs first in priority.

1. diagnosis of needs
2. formulation of objectives
3. selection of content
4. organization of content
5. selection of learning experiences
6. organization of learning experiences
7. evaluation

Essentially, the process is the same as Tyler's except for the inclusion of the diagnosis of needs, and what I think is the redundant selection and organization of content prior to learning experiences.

The emphasis on objectives also brought together previously antithetical groups: the humanists and the growing number of behavioralists. Objectives clarified ambiguous purposes in the humanities, and for the behavioralists sharpened what was expected of students to observable performance, and not aspects of thinking or appreciation that were vague and unspecified.

The development of objectives, by itself and without reference to a particular point of departure, does not solve the curricular dilemma. Writing performance-based objectives, no matter how specific, does not respond to the question of philosophical origin. Developing objectives presumes a response to the question, based on what premise? My own preferences are that curriculum development must proceed from developmental student needs, both biological and psychological, and must also take into consideration wide fluctuations in individual differences in ability and development over time for an individual, and for differing student populations. Consequently, curriculum goals must include aspects of commonality in the curriculum and provide for instances of diversity in performance among individuals.

Robert Mager's *Preparing Instructional Objectives* was a cornerstone book from its publication date in 1962 in reshaping American education. It was short, very readable, easy to understand and practical in clarifying a teacher's goals and perspective. It was exactly the sort of primer necessary to teach people how to write objectives. Mager made it clear that his book was not about a philosophy of education, nor about who should select objectives nor which objectives should be used. Mager's intent was to help teachers write "meaningful stated objectives," but it was clear they were to be performance based in reference to goals. The ethos of performance as a measurement for curriculum progress received a renewed thrust and became standard vocabulary for educators. The performance objectives movement became a campaign for increased writing clarity, but hesitated in incorporating adolescent needs into curriculum planning. The performance or competency-based movement, while sound in many respects, often seemed to ignore that every instrument existed to measure all kinds of schooling performance and student achievement. Although there are scores of cognitive level tests, tests which measure emotional states are in limited supply.

Individual teachers and entire schools may have developed lists of behavioral objectives for students. Yet these comprehensive lists may have little bearing on established schooling goals, which brings us to the relationship of schooling and curriculum goals.

SCHOOLING GOALS AND CURRICULUM ENDS

For most practical purposes, definitions of "goals" and of "objectives" are synonymous, although a goal is something to be reached, and an objective is the expenditure of energy and purpose towards an end. I use "goal" as an institutional or schooling terminus, and "objective" as steps towards achieving goals.

Goodlad's study of American schools has demonstrated that most educators agree that schools should provide for the general areas of academic, social, vocational and personal advancement universally for all students. However, the difference between intent and practice is wide. Goodlad's extensive survey showed that schools pay little attention to the balance of curriculum offerings to meet these schooling goals. And there appeared to be no consensus on what constitutes the core of the curriculum.

It might be helpful to look at the goals for one senior American high school to see what they include.

1. To encourage a desire for academic excellence.
2. Develop a sense of moral and ethical values.
3. Encourage a sense of social and physical development and interaction.
4. Encourage the development of an understanding of emotional feelings and how to remain in control.
5. Encourage an appreciation for the fine arts.
6. Develop a sense of value for the democratic structure of government and the free enterprise system.
7. Help each student become better prepared as a self-sustaining, productive member of society through effective teaching and effective counseling.

Such goal statements exist as in a dream-state, quite apart from practical reality, and they are in no way related to course design, curricular content, and teacher evaluation. Nor do schools seem to hold themselves accountable for whether or not students actually fulfill these lofty ambitions, and to what degree. Similar statements of goals will be repeated in secondary schools in all industrial countries. The wording, and certainly the syntax, will vary but the main themes will all be there. In this school's statement there is a confusion between what the school expects, and does, and what is expected of the student. The subject of each sentence is unclear.

But more pertinent to the discussion here is that these schooling goals can be developed by the principal or school head independent of the existing curricula. Or, conceived another way, a new secondary school could be built and the curricula in place when someone remembers that for accreditation purposes a school philosophy and goals need to be written. What doesn't exist is a clear and logical extension of the curriculum ends extending from schooling goals. Hence, refined student performance objectives can be developed in exacting detail but they might be only peripherally related to the school's institutional and curricular requirements for graduation.

Somewhere in our collective haste to build schools for an expanding population after World War II, and our concern for fiscal restraint and quality in the teaching staff, we lost sight of the crucial transition from general to limited purpose: from school goals to curriculum means. We perfected our objectives for student activities, and constricted our understanding of schooling purposes upon which the curriculum should rest.

Goodlad has outlined schooling goals as a result of his massive "Study of Schooling," as described in *A Place Called School* (1984). I present a condensed listing:

ACADEMIC GOALS
   1. Mastery of Basic Skills and Fundamental Processes
      a) read, write, communicate, do arithmetic
      b) get new ideas
      c) use math
      d) use information

   2. Intellectual Development
      a) develop a general knowledge base

      d) develop positive attitudes

VOCATIONAL GOALS
   1. Building a Career
      a) selecting an occupation
      b) making decisions about work
      c) develop salable skills and special knowledge
      d) develop work habits
      e) attitudes toward work

SOCIAL AND CULTURAL GOALS
   1. Interpersonal Relationships
      a) understanding different opinions and values
      b) understanding basic family patterns
      c) develop group skills
      d) develop ability to advance others' concerns
      e) form satisfying relationships
      f) concern for humanity, international relations
      g) concern for different cultures

   2. Citizenship

   3. Enculturation

   4. Moral and Ethical Character

PERSONAL GOALS
   1. Emotional and Physical Well-being
      a) expand emotional capacity
      b) skills for adjustment, change
      c) knowledge of one's body; good health
      d) leisure time use
      e) physical fitness; recreational skills
      f) self-criticism

2. Creativity and Aesthetic Expression
   a) deal with problems in new ways
   b) tolerance
   c) flexible or different points of view
   d) evaluate expression
   e) communicate through creativity
   f) contribute to cultural life

These are comprehensive schooling goals and the action required is to translate them into curriculum units, where they don't presently exist, and to ensure some coordination and continuity in purpose. When I discuss goals with teachers as the building blocks for curriculum, the response I get when I point out that most are not "classes" taught is that such goals are already being taught in all classes. It is a perfectly understandable defense mechanism. But when I ask for the evidence of satisfactory accomplishment, of say social and cultural and personal goals fulfillment, of course there is none, neither in the paper and pencil tests teachers devise, in the school's tests, or in standardized national tests. The myth that all teachers can do all things to all students under all conditions is deeply entrenched, although often denied.

SCHOOL INHIBITORS OF CURRICULUM INTEGRATION

It is the structure of schooling imperatives that dominates the curriculum process: the hardware seems to dictate the software, and not the opposite. The division of school levels, age groupings, subject groupings and specific subjects are the greatest determinants of curriculum flexibility. Indeed, among most graduate students and practicing educators it is very difficult to begin an understanding of curriculum development apart from presently existing curricula. The process of education cannot easily be abstracted from current schooling means.

And yet to begin a process of curriculum development is to begin afresh, without the preconceptions of what now exists. It is to think like a scientist approaching a puzzle and to re-conceptualize the framework for supporting the discovery of knowledge. It is to ask new questions (or old ones imperfectly answered or never asked) like, "what do we want students to be able to do when they finish schooling?"

A quote from Aristotle is appropriate here:

> It is clear that there should be legislation about education and that it should be conducted on a public system...What constitutes education and what is the proper way to be educated. At present there are differences of opinion as to be proper tasks to be set; for all people do not agree as to the things that the young ought to learn...nor is it clear whether their studies should be regulated more with regard to intellect or with regard to character. And confusing questions arise out of the education that actually prevails, and it is not clear whether the pupils should practice pursuits that are practically useful, or morally edifying, or higher accomplishments-- for all these views win the support of some judges; and nothing is agreed upon as regards the exercises of virtue, for, to start with, all men do not honor the same virtue, so

that they naturally hold different opinions in regard to
training in virtue.

Politics, VIII, 2

What is startling about this quotation is how contemporary it sounds, as if no progress has been made since the middle of the third century B.C. in resolving the central purposes of schooling. What should the young learn? What teaching activities should there be? Should schools stress intellectual or character development? If students are to learn virtue, whose virtue? Aristotle goes to the heart of the schooling problem and discusses the curriculum issues--what should students learn and what should they be taught.

But Aristotle considered education as a part of politics, and in my view it is the established political structure--the national and state laws, the rules and regulations, the institutionalization and organization of schooling--that in its rigidity to change and use of orthodox methods constrains flexible curriculum development. The organizing structure of the facility of the school, the classroom organization, age grading, and subject dominance combine to inhibit curriculum integration.

Curriculum decisions and practices are developed in the absence of an educational philosophy. At one extreme such decisions are limited to the purchase of texts. In a flurry of intense curriculum exercises, scores of objectives and activities are devised for individual student performance. In a quiet and reflective moment, an administrator writes out a short list of the school goals and an accompanying statement expressing its philosophy. What students actually think about what they're learning, how they integrate it now in a meaningful way, may never be known because no one asks them. In any event, the results of such a survey would never form the foundation for schooling in publicly supported schools.

CURRICULUM AS PROGRAM

We have seen that man incessantly presents
individual differences in all parts of his body
and in his mental faculties.
Charles Darwin, *The Descent Of Man*

What do you want the student to be able to do or know 1) after the material has been taught (or self-learned); and 2) to be ready to learn subsequent material or content? Each examination of content in reality forms the basis for another level of learning, either in depth within the subject, or as transfer across subjects. Thus, assessment of any kind is a demonstration of competence and of growth, and an evaluation of readiness for further study. And it is presumably grounded in some kind of educational philosophy about student growth and development, and the proper balance between knowledge, skills and attitudes to be developed.

The curriculum model I propose here does not focus on academic subject matter as its main referent, although growth in intellectual development and in knowledge is a major consideration. Instead, the main point of departure is grounded in the individual, on the development process consistent with normal biological development. Academic subjects become only one of the means for attaining progressive personal and intellectual growth.

In 1938, the National Education Association in the U.S. proposed in its booklet, *The Purposes Of Education In American Democracy* , four major goals for schools: self-realization, human relationships, economic efficiency and civic responsibility. These goals were considered appropriate for all levels of students. Note that two of the goals are personal and two relate to society or the state. These are reasonable schooling goals, but schools have rarely derived curricular decisions based on such noble institutional objectives. Instead, curriculum decisions are most often made in the absence of a constructive philosophy.

I suggest for reflective consideration, first, the development of guiding constructs which will serve as schooling goals. I propose three principal constructs for curriculum, all based on personal development:

personal: what the person learns, how he or she grows intellectually, physically, ethically and aesthetically

social: how the person interacts with others

practical and productive: what the individual does, what he or she produces, how he or she lives

These curriculum constructs are intended to provide major intellectual guides for curriculum synthesis and exploration of areas of study. They are intended to help integrate, for the young person, school subjects, customarily cordoned off from each other in tight but discrete particles to be learned, for which there is often little student perceived relevance.

Why can't there be a teacher of social interaction skills for example, instead of just an eighth grade teacher, or an English teacher? If schooling goals are paramount, and not subject demands, then why can't teachers be responsible for whole domains of student growth and not just subjects? Would it take inspired leadership to administratively assign teachers, as their primary instructional responsibility, to major schooling goals?

I have not used the conventional taxonomies of school learning-- cognitive, affective and psychomotor--primarily because I believe that each of these is not biologically related, and that the distinctions are somewhat artificial and not completely distinct properties. They are philosophical distinctions upon which a whole series of schooling objectives have been designed. Furthermore, these classification systems were designed principally as means of developing curriculum objectives and do not address the problem of personal involvement in learning.

I believe that significant learning occurs when the learner can perceive the relevance of the knowledge encounter. What is the curriculum content for a student who suddenly declares, "I hate math"? What is the proper educational objective the math teacher should pursue at this point? Does the student really hate the subject, or the teacher, or the school, or studying? And how does the math teacher distinguish? Because schooling is compulsory, interest in schooling or in particular subjects is not debatable, and teachers defend themselves against such rude questions as best they can, and often with limited success.

The greatest curriculum deficiency that I presently perceive in schools is the absence of taught social skills. Ask a normal adult what is most important in life and the response I find most common is "human relationships." Some of the most significant human problems concern how we interact with each other. Basic communications skills are essential to a fulfilling life, and yet are absent from the formal curriculum. We choose people to marry, to have children with, to raise children, to work with. Yet these crucial skills in human interaction, despite protestations about school as a preparation for life, are rarely to be found in standard curricula. Why? Because the social development of children

47

and youth, even if statements exist in a school's goals, never gets translated into the "academic" arena. Social development, and especially social interaction skills, is not a customary schooling subject. I believe that these constructs can be developed into a set of realistic schooling goals. As Bobbitt said in *The Curriculum* in 1918: "The teacher must see the serious ends in order to adjust conditions, to control motives, and to guide." I believe that these constructs can form the foundation for a curriculum core. My idea for a secondary school curriculum is the mutual exploration by teachers and students of a few important ideas.

But I realize that for most schools this is a quantum leap into the risky unknown, and so I propose a transition that includes a more structured program of studies.

AN ALTERNATIVE PROGRAM OF STUDIES

The proposed program of studies is the outline of the curriculum goals: personal, social and practical. The goals are embodied in the constructs. The program of studies is the formalization of the curriculum domains. Its primary intent is to build the skills necessary to satisfy the goals. The study program, with its emphasis on traditional subjects, is the means of achieving the schooling goals. Here let me quote Bobbitt again:

> The curriculum-discoverer will first be an analyst of
> human nature and human affairs. His task at this point
> is not at all concerned with "the studies,"--later he will
> draw up appropriate studies as *Means*--but he will not
> analyze the tools to be used in a piece of work as a mode
> of discovering the objectives of that work.

Bobbitt's last sentence here is a little confusing, but I understand it to mean that curriculum developers will not confuse the subjects of schooling with schooling ends; they will not analyze the subject tools as if they were educational objectives. Schooling goals will emerge from an analysis of "human nature and human affairs." Given the custodial nature of schools and the laws protecting the young, students cannot roam freely seeking community experiences. The kinds of "experiences" progressive educators spoke about are still available, but since the proliferation of vicarious experiences via the existing media, students can now be exposed literally to the world. The amount of available material on nearly all subjects in print, on film, video cassette, film strips and audio cassettes is prodigious. Visual home entertainment systems have expanded enormously, as home video movies transform public habits. What is needed is the same accessibility for schools of learning material by the latest technology.

With the accumulation of pertinent learning resources in mind, the program of studies, based on the educational constructs, I suggest is this:

1) intellectual skills: reading, math, philosophy, history
2) social and communicative skills: interpersonal relations, ethics and morals, languages
3) physical skills: health, physical fitness, recreation, sports, leisure
4) aesthetic arts: literature, poetry, art, music, drama, cinema, photography
5) natural and physical sciences: biology, chemistry, physics
6) practical arts and sciences: geography, engineering, domestic sciences

This proposed program of studies does not assume that the existing courses are taught under a new rubric or classification. What it presumes is a new way of thinking about what is intended for human development purposes in schools. That is why the program emphasizes the acquisition of skills, and not just the expansion of knowledge, and why the concept of, for example, the aesthetic appreciation does not begin with a subject but a gestalt exploration of the world of perceived beauty.

A century ago, the educated gentleman needed Greek. It was his badge of having gone to school, his credential for success. The text he studied made this clear, as a popular book in the 1830s makes clear:

> In the use of this Grammar, it would be adviseable that
> the attention of the young student should be first called
> to those parts of it which have an immediate bearing upon
> his studies, and that, upon a second and third revisal, he
> should be taken in succession over those portions which
> might tend to embarrass him in the commencement of
> his career.

The graduate of preparatory schools had to demonstrate the contents of school learning. Showing off what he had learned was the admission ticket into polite and genteel society. And school books were the primary vehicle of the transmission of concepts valued by literate society. Going through them was a ritual and form of character development. One became a man by taking Latin and Greek and Mathematics. Thus, intellectual and character development were mutually reinforcing by taking difficult subjects. A quote from a book on geometry published in 1819 makes this implication.

> In school-books, and those designed for the use of
> learners, it has always appeared to me, that plain and
> concise rules, with proper exercises, are entirely
> sufficient for the purpose; it being obvious that example
> in science, as well as in morals, will always inforce
> and illustrate precept.

A student became tough in character by encountering tough subjects. Students might have argued that the stiffening in resolution was not necessarily in favor of subject enthusiasm.

The graphic I have included with this section illustrates the potential diversity of relations between each curriculum construct--personal, social, practical and productive--to teaching method. For example, if I am teaching ethical development among adolescents, which is the predominate teaching method to use--lecture, discussion, independent study, laboratory, or some other method? If I use all these methods in combination, which is most appropriate for satisfying the criterion? Similarly, if I am teaching writing, which teaching method is better suited to the goal of improved writing competence?

In teaching the curriculum it is relatively easy to fall into the habit of maintaining the same teaching method without variation regardless of the circumstance. The skillful instructor varies the instructional method with the goal to be attained, and does not allow the method of teaching to become routine and to interfere with realistic student progress. Using this format or a similar one permits curriculum developers to suggest possible percentages of total time by teaching method for each major schooling goal. The introduction of teaching methods directly into the curriculum model also suggests that the educational leadership is concerned with the

TEACHING METHODS

EXAMPLES OF SCHOOLING GOALS OR LEARNING OBJECTIVES	lecture	discussion	independent study	laboratory session
I Personal intellectual skills development attitudes & motivation moral & ethical development etc.				
II Social interpersonal skills social values etc.				
III Practical & Productive writing musical training building artifacts etc.				

experimental use by teachers of flexible methods for goal attainment.

The teaching methods included here are not exhaustive. As I noted in the chapter on the instructing act, the methods also include grouping practices, technical skills, and the management of instruction, as well as teaching style and the diagnosis of learning ability.

The business of secondary schools is teaching school subjects, that is what it has always been and will likely continue to be despite continued cries for reform and flexibility in its *modus operandi*. The label of a school subject is supposed to be the justification for its continued existence. When you do the subject, you do school. Covering the material is equivalent to completing an education.

After all (as the traditional argument for justification of the status quo goes), there isn't any time to do anything else. And thus time, as a simple variable for manipulation, becomes the barrier for adaptability. Obviously nothing new can be done because there isn't time for it in the schedule. There is no integration of subjects, and little synthesis of areas of learning. Subjects are given and received in random order, as a typical student moves through the day in literature, algebraic formulae, conjugating French verbs, and memorizing the reasons why America entered the World War I--all before lunch break. The discrepancy between schooling goals and subject matter procedures is wide, and goals like "critical thinking skills development," or "realizing full potential" never quite get incorporated into the curriculum units. The rhetorical documents about educational purposes are tolerated as worthy, but in fact are inaccurate representations of actual schooling practice.

As one American western state says in a state law, teachers shall develop:

> ...common honesty, morality, courtesy, obedience
> to law...respect for parents and home, the dignity
> and necessity of honest labor, and other skills, habits
> and qualities of character which will promote an
> upright and desirable citizenry and which will better
> prepare our youth for a richer happier life.

These legal schooling goals are often instruction for character, not intellectual or social, development. The question is, where can an independent observer see them in the curriculum, which Ted Sizer calls "a cauldron of polemics."

Students can be a burden to society when they leave school and can't find work. But while in school, they are off the streets, out of the labor market, supervised by competent adults, and, presumably, learning something.

A program of studies is like a catechism of belief. It is a helpful classification system for progressing through a learning adventure if no other plan exists. My own preference for learning with adolescents (and, by the by, with experienced teachers) is to develop a new plan: to rearrange the taxonomies; to create a Rubik's cube; to explore what is already known within and redefine it; and then to seek out the uncharted territory and find the missing answers. In this sense, existing curricula are merely ornamental to the pursuit of self learning. In fact, the more particular and specific the lesson plan, the more remote the distance from schooling goals.

PART TWO:

CURRICULUM PRACTICES

The belief that a curriculum can be devised and kept relevant to the present is an illusion: whose present, in the first place, and relevant for how long? Students differ in tastes, knowledge, and emotional orientation. What concerns (or "excites") one four-year generation will bore the next, as anyone can verify by reference to popular music. And so it is with literature, politics, and the current view of creeds and crises.

Jacques Barzun, *The American University*

Chapter Five

A MINORITY GROUP CURRICULUM MODEL:
AN AMERICAN INDIAN EXAMPLE

In the United States, minority education has a turbulent but well-documented history. Nearly every industrialized country and most developing nations have resident minority populations whose presence in schools often serves as a challenge to educators and to the transmission of a homogeneous culture. Contemporary curriculum increasingly involves controversy about programs for the culturally or ethnically different among majority school populations.

Minority groups, either for political or religious reasons, sometimes seek to gain control of the education of their children because the formal, institutionalized bureaucracy of the school has been unwilling or unable to accommodate minority cultural interests and needs (or worse, denigrates those particular needs). Moreover, the curriculum often ignores the value of minority participation in the content of the subject and in the learning process.

Although certain modifications will always be welcomed in cafeteria and food services, dress codes, and arrangements for religious services on special occasions, I am suggesting in this chapter the need for curriculum accommodation, for the development of appropriate alternatives to content and approaches to minority learning needs. This is not so much a question, then, of special techniques of curriculum design as it is an attitudinal determination to use curriculum content or learning activities as a means for accelerating skill development, and to base school learning in differentiated cultural contexts.

The ethnic minority group in the U.S. that has had the greatest popular and professional interest has been numerically the smallest population group--the American Indian, comprising less than one percent of the total U.S. population. This chapter is an analysis of a curriculum model for American Indian schools I developed based on my experiences with both western and eastern American Indian groups, and in public school systems with large numbers of American Indian students. I offer it as an example of a culturally relevant curriculum model useful for the culturally different, as a school or program model.

I have used in the model's development cultural anthropology as a social science method. I chose cultural anthropology because I want to emphasize not new ventures for structuring the content of schooling to allow minority groups alternatives, but as a means for minority groups to find outlets for cultural expression within the curriculum. In a world where White is a minority, it is imperative to cultivate new attitudes, a new way of conceiving of the curriculum and the content of what we pass on to the next generation. Cultural anthropology, as a social science approach, offers a unique dimension to curriculum development.

In 1965, Jerome Bruner and his associates began the development of the broad outlines of what later became a major curriculum innovation. It was known as *Man: A Course Of Study*, and was conceived as a means of teaching children the role of human beings in the total environment and mankind's relation to the animal world. The questions Bruner asked were these:

> What is human about human beings?
> How did they get that way?
> How can they be made more so?

Bruner noted then: "We seek exercises and materials through which our pupils can learn wherein man is distinctive in his adaptation to the world, and wherein there is a discernible continuity between him and his animal forbears." The content of this curriculum focus was animal behavior from the salmon to baboons and a migratory Eskimo people called the Netsilik. Curriculum themes were the life cycle, life patterns, and how organic life develops in a hostile environment. The intellectual and pedagogical assumptions that underlie the development of this unique curriculum package also form the basis for this curriculum model for minorities, and is rooted in the same anthropological concerns.

THE AMERICAN INDIAN IN EDUCATION

Unknown even to most Americans, American Indians live in all 50 states, speak over 300 different tribal languages, and are extraordinarily diverse among tribal groups and between tribal "nations." Contrary to popular misunderstanding, over 50 percent do not live on federal reservations. The largest concentration of American Indians is now in the major urban centers: New York, Chicago, Milwaukee, Philadelphia, Minneapolis, to name a few.

As early as 1842 there were 37 American Indian boarding schools administered by the then new Bureau of Indian Affairs created by the War Department. The misguided policy was to undermine the culture of American Indians by forcing a disciplined and restrictive schooling within a boarding or missionary environment. Many of these schools still exist. The intent was to strip the American Indian of his culture and to substitute the English language and American "civilization," however ill-defined, in its place. The social and cultural disintegration of the family quickly followed these misconceived and unwisely applied policies.

After more than a century of federal control, the most enlightening and lively process of change among western, reservation Indians and tribes is decentralization. Local autonomy in tribal affairs, and community control of even Bureau of Indian Affairs schools, is a recent phenomenon. The particular situation depends upon previous treaty arrangments with the U.S. government, state legislation, and tribal laws. Native schools in other countries--the Bantu schools in South Africa and the Aboriginal schools in Australia come to mind--have similar problems with local vs. state or federal control. The issue of local control of schools for separate native groups, especially when the native group has laws governing education, is not as inflammatory as that of separate education for immigrant minority groups, or even of separate religious schools. In the U.S. there cannot be separate schools for Polish or Irish or Blacks or Asians--this is unconstitutional--as there can for American Indians because the U.S. government does not have treaty obligations with other minorities as it does with American Indians. Local control for American Indians has devolved from a time when tribes were dealt with as separate nations, conquered, as it were, on their own territory. But the treaties for those tribes, where they apply, are still legally binding.

The Navajos are the largest American Indian nation in the U.S. Their reservation comprises about 16 million acres straddling northeastern Arizona, northwestern New Mexico, and southern Utah. It is roughly the size of Wales. Almost all Navajo children speak Navajo at home, and negligible English, if any, when they come to school. Language difficulties are only foremost among their beginning learning problems. Many Bureau of Indian Affairs schools, once operated by the government, are now contracted out to local authorities.

These contract schools, like other locally controlled schools, are now confronting basic curriculum decisions about cultural relevance and academic excellence. Preparing a child completely in the culture may not lead to occupational or even cultural acceptance in the world beyond the reservation. On the other hand, maintaining only traditional, so-called Anglo, curriculum units does not endear the Indian school to the Indian community. The key is to find a curriculum balance that blends some cultural relevance with accepted academic quality.

Many urban schools with large American Indian student populations have tried to accommodate cultural differences with federal aid. Some large school systems, like those in Seattle, Tacoma, Oakland, Chicago and Tulsa, have established alternative school programs based on Indian customs. The problem for the curriculum planner is how to take advantage of the minority cultural ways of learning while simultaneously teaching important aspects of the dominant culture.

To pretend to educate while ignoring ancestry, background, language and personal history is psychologically unsound and educationally unreasonable. Everyone assimilates a culture, and uses the culture to gain new knowledge.

CULTURAL IDENTITY AND THE CURRICULUM

Only for the dominant culture has the school been the place where a people's children have found their cultural identity. However, there are many elements which can be incorporated within a curriculum plan which can illustrate the diversity of the human family. Explorations into other cultures can be intimidating for teachers unwilling to challenge their own misgivings or risk learning as they ask their students to do.

A search for a cultural identity is not necessarily a confrontation with Western civilization. Unfortunately, requests for curriculum and schooling changes to accommodate differences are often the result of communities intellectually isolated, by choice, from wider contact in the world, and unwilling to admit these differences into their neighborhoods. Prejudicial parents, not the children themselves, are the main cause for the lack of global understanding.

I believe that the first priority for a minority culture within a school is the writing of elementary texts by minority representatives explaining the elements of the culture paramount for the young to know. The process for this curriculum development of short, illustrated books easily digested by children can be extensive if the entire minority community is involved, not just individuals who can put together written materials. These home developed books will then form the basis for a continual process of curriculum development for all children in learning about a particular culture.

A general outline for an American Indian curriculum might look like this:

1. Description of the Family
   a) role of parents
   b) role of children
   c) sibling relationships
   d) role of relatives
   e) relation of family to community or tribe

2. Description of Community
   a) role of elders and leaders
   b) community activities
   c) ceremonial and religious functions
   d) marriages, births and deaths

3. The Relation of Community to Nation
   a) relations between communities
   b) religious vs. national relations
   c) country of residence vs. country of origin

Besides general and perhaps historical descriptions of the minority culture, specific short texts might include daily activities such as the choice and preparation of food. Specific topics could include: the choice of food--for religious purposes, for example; fasting or food abstinence; foods for festive occasions; nutritional value; etc.

The introduction of a specific curriculum unit can often serve as a vehicle for re-thinking the delivery of the curriculum. A possible approach is thematic, whereby under the traditional social studies heading individual units could include broader themes such as: law and governance among peoples; the family; modes of education; food gatherings and eating practices; beliefs and sacred ceremonies. The advantage of minority curriculum units developed by minority cultures is that they are appropriate to all students, not just the dominant majority. All students will need to know about the shrinking world in which they will live. The curriculum, like the school's philosophy and programs, should broaden not constrict this sense of global understanding.

A tribal or community group can also begin to develop a documented history of its own. Some minority groups, and certainly American Indians, resent the presence of anthropologists in their midst. The idea here is for the culturally distinct group to document its own history and culture that goes beyond the oral tradition. What does the minority community find threatening in the majority culture? What elements of the culture must remain intact, without change or compromise, and which can be modified? How can the minority culture remain within a majority culture and yet be culturally distinctive? How can these differences be reflected in the curriculum? The answers may involve differentiating the community group from a larger national group in another country, or a tribal group from a larger community. An Asian immigrant may feel isolated from the central culture and threatened by absorption and cultural loss. The attempt to document even the immigrant history will help restore the sense of control over the educative process.

ASSUMPTIONS ABOUT CURRICULUM PLANNING
FOR MINORITY CULTURES

I have made several assumptions about curriculum planning for American Indian schools that I think are also appropriate for other minority cultures. These assumptions are not necessarily unique to minority learning.

1. That the curriculum for minority children be planned around the motivation and interest levels of the children and youth.
"All men by nature desire to know," wrote Aristotle in the *Metaphysics.* But some educators may question whether the love of learning is an acquired taste, or a teachable attitude, or both. But whether student motivation and interest is genetic, or determined by the class environment, or generated by the individual, self motivation is psychologically the chief ingredient in successful learning. The educator who plans curriculum units around existing interest levels finds a receptive audience.

2. That the central role of the curriculum is to develop the child's capabilities to improve learning skills.
The object of this psychological assumption is not only to encourage a student to change behavior as a result of experience, but also to learn the skills that will increase the capacity to learn. This is obviously not an assumption that encourages repeated acts of memorization, and the recall of simple facts. Cognitively, it assumes high order skills like application, synthesis, and evaluation. The curriculum's content should reflect skill development in learning, not just factual detail.

3. That assessment of student progress be based largely on individual performance towards a criterion, and not primarily normative references.
Clearly, a student who is, let's say, a recent immigrant from an Asian country, whose language in the vernacular is limited, and whose progress in formal schooling minimal, cannot in fairness be measured on standardized achievement or aptitude tests without considerable scepticism over the results. The language developments and ability in the new language would tend to skew the results negatively, regardless of innate ability. The curriculum progress of minority children will vary widely in spite of equivalency in age, sex or other schooling factors. In practice, attention to minority children's needs is often represented in remedial programs as if something were wrong with the children and not the curriculum. Grading and evaluation must be somewhat personalized to specific goals that may be unique for individuals, not the whole class. Merely improving scores through continual practice is not the goal, but the interaction of new behaviors with past responses: the transfer of learned experiences to new situations.

4. That the total curriculum in the preparatory stages be environmentally oriented.
The North American native has a deep and abiding reverence for all of nature, all living things. It is a genuine characteristic of people who live close to the soil and the earth. The American Indian, for example, is patient with the living earth, and knows that it cannot be technologically be disturbed without damage. This special view of the world is a new discovery for modern man, and the impact of environmental erosion--

of the gradual disappearance of natural and irreplaceable resources--is not uniformly understood throughout the world.

The sense of mystery and awe that permeates the present and past of native groups can easily become a permanent thematic feature of the curriculum. This thematic approach characterizes this particular curriculum case study. The land, the water, the production and storage of food, wind--these elemental forces can themselves be the basis for curriculum planning units. Social studies can be an investigation between the natural environment and the man-made environment. Examples could be the food chain, states of energy, the animal world, and so on.

Schools have so succumbed to academic subjects that it is difficult to revise thinking to consider what else can be the content of curriculum apart from them. A study of the environment is not just science, or social studies, or math. My own view is that school subjects are means to learning, not ends. The focus of the curriculum can be any legitimate field of inquiry. I am suggesting that the focus of curriculum for minority students begin with questions about the world around them.

FURTHER PSYCHOLOGICAL ASSUMPTIONS

There are scores of ways a child can learn about his or her culture and other cultures. I suggest that the use in the curriculum of a few psychologically sound guides for improving learning will be helpful in all contexts. Some of the ways children can learn best are:

* by muscular and psychomotor or biological association.

For example, an American Indian who executes a dance routine for performance in a ceremony will tend to remember the traditions of the ceremony more if engaged in the actual performance. A child will learn to play volleyball better through playing it than by listening to a teacher talk about the rules. All this seems simple enough, but not enough curriculum is based on actual movement. Physical movement is one of the strongest forms of memory association.

* by doing

When a child is taught the fine art of fishing, he or she learns best through experience. The "doing" presumes action. It presumes directions have been given and understood, and simple psychomotor skills developed so that a complex series of acts can be executed. Children need to "do" the curriculum more.

* by symbolic association

Symbols represent the culture, a people, the forces which help preserve a way of life. A sacred mountain, a valley, a house of a pioneer, a flag, a star--each sign in a particular culture has a value. The geography of place has a deep meaning to a people, like political refugees, who can no longer go home. This sense of roots is important to the content of the curriculum for minorities.

* by dramatization

Acting out is a strong form of cultural learning. There are scores of stories in every culture which encapsulate its past. Story-telling and the imaginative power of myth in a culture can be a prelude to drama. Pantomime is another rich source of dramatic acting. Children love to dress up and perform. Each curriculum unit can include examples of play acting a story, a life scene, an interaction. The playing of roles helps the children learn another dimension or perspective, and is a powerful learning tool.

* by trial

Sometimes it is painful to learn, and lessons that need to be learned come with difficulty. Although no curriculum should be an endurance contest, there may be some units which require exhibitions of physical trial and mental concentration. The use of a physical trial to prove ability may seem primitive. Yet it is the essence of the Olympics and the games which stress higher, faster, and farther. In many cultures, passing a physical trial proves manhood and is the admissions test into adult society: stalking and killing a boy's first deer, or the Walkabout among Aboriginals in Australia. If a culture stresses the necessity of some form of trial for both the young man and young woman, the curriculum should make some provision. The passing of a young person through puberty is too often ignored by the formal curriculum; the school is not much help in assisting the transition into adulthood. Older cultures have defined times and events which determine when a young boy becomes a man.

* by art

The cultivation of the aesthetic is much neglected in modern schooling. Yet children can learn much when they physically manipulate a paint brush, a musical instrument, clay, or create forms from inanimate substances. Art develops the right brain, and adds balance to the blackboard paralysis of the classroom. The joy of discovery, of making something seemingly from nothing, adds to a child's heightened motivation. The curriculum can always point out where the beauty lies in all things, and let the student experiment with new forms.

The total curriculum content and delivery is supposed to be an aid in the development of meaning for the minority student learning to live in an "alien" culture, the dominant group culture, while learning his or her own. A minority student must simultaneously learn two cultures, perhaps two languages, two sets of responses, two perspectives on the world. One cultural response may be antithetical to the other. But a curriculum approach that is sympathetic to the wide and diversified range of cultures is a beginning towards the development of a positive attitude in children. No culture has all the answers, and all cultures can learn from each other. Curriculum can lead the way in the reduction and elimination of bias and prejudice in color, language, race, ethnic group, nationality, and religion.

I have suggested that the total scope of the curriculum be the theme of the environment. I do not mean that this be limited to the mineral, vegetative, and animal world, but also the interactive world of the child in the environment. This is neither geography, anthropology, sociology, science or social studies. To understand the role of content in the curriculum, I believe it is necessary to back away from the traditional school subjects. Creating curriculum units for minority children and youth is one way to build on a new perspective for conceptualizing the curriculum.

CURRICULAR CONCEPTS

The anthropologist studies patterns of behavior, and ways in which a people change or remain constant, their culture. My own simplistic definition of culture is what a people do, or how they act. This includes their traditions, beliefs, values, skills and knowledge. For the purposes of this example of curriculum development, culture is an important concept. The other key concepts are environment, and the man-made environment.

Discussions, map study, films, material development can all supplement a topical outline like the following list:

physical needs: food , shelter, clothing, transportation,
communication, recreation, technology

social needs: education, government

spiritual needs: values, beliefs

social environment: language groups, tribal, ethnic,
national, global

The central themes might be:

1) man in the physical environment
2) social control: the group and the individual
3) civilization

This kind of curriculum, designed around topical themes and rooted in culture, gives a broader structural understanding to student learning. It is pedagogically uneconomical to teach topics without clarifying context. It is the understanding of principles that assists generalization and transfer of learning. Facts learned apart from a context are also more likely to be forgotten.

THE ENVIRONMENT AS CURRICULUM THEME

The world of flora and fauna, of wind and weather, and of natural elements and animals, is viewed differently in the world's cultures. The value of rain, for example, in an agricultural area is undisputed. But rain may also have a spirit meaning, a transcendental value that supercedes the natural phenomenon. The cultural value of a natural occurrence may be more important than its scientific description. American Indian tribes throughout the American West have dances for the eagle, coyote, deer, and buffalo. It is the distinctly cultural values of the ethnic or minority group that the curriculum should seek to convey by means of the environment as a curricular theme.

In American and European society property forms a societal priority. Who owns the environment? In one sense, it is a frivolous question. But since the advent of acid rain, environmental pollution in the air and in oceans has given the lie to the safeguards of national and economic interests. The American Indian regards the earth as his mother. No one can possibly own it in a personal sense, and this native view of the land transcends political boundaries and exploitative interests. Hence, concern for the preservation of the earth and its properties is a form of self-preservation and self-interest.

If we assume that the environment in its broadest sense is the overall theme of curriculum planning, then I suggest that the principles of academic orientation be grouped around the following means of understanding:

I Energy and Matter

This thematic unit could consist of math, and the physical and natural sciences.

II Language and Culture

This curriculum grouping would allow for instruction in language, the social sciences and social studies, broadly understood.

III Spirit and Life

This unit is organized around art and literature, poetry, religion (where possible) and the exploration of unique ways of human belief and understanding.

IV Law and Economics

Under this unit students would study the development of consumer skills, the management of money and resources, and the roots of law and government.

V Physical Development and Health

This unit helps develop the student's psychomotor skills and talents, and emotional and mental health capabilities.

These five curriculum units encompass most of the traditional academic course offerings, but they are subsumed under more meaningful categories for learning. I believe that they can provide, with the context of the theme of a study of the environment, an integrated and unified approach to knowledge and cultural assimilation. In this context, schooling subjects become, as they should always be viewed, as means to the total development of the person, and not as specific goals of instruction in themselves.

Moreover, these curriculum units can be taught sequentially over long periods of time--several years for example--or they can be taught intensely, for example one year at a time. But the assumption should not necessarily be that each unit or broad concept be given equal treatment or all taught for the same length of time. Some students might explore some units more in detail than others. Clearly, on another level of schooling, it is possible to obtain doctoral degrees in any of these areas. On a school preparatory level, all students should have explored all the broad areas in some detail. The units are not necessarily geared to earning a living or obtaining work.

Students can spend time exploring and studying the natural environment of a region or alternatively, describe one they cannot visually verify. The natural environment shapes where and how a people live and what they do to survive. A second study unit could revolve around responses to the question of how neighboring groups lived within a region.

And a third unit could be designed around responses to how groups reacted or react to the intrusion of other groups in their territories--of the reaction of natives groups to European settlers in America or Australia, or the reaction of Europeans to immigrant settlers from Asia.

EXAMPLE OF A TEACHING-LEARNING UNIT

Assuming the environment as the central theme, what might a specific curriculum unit contain, let's say in the general category of Energy and Matter? This broad area could include math and measurement, and the physical and natural sciences, but its principal goal would be skill development in solving problems relating to how a person lives in and confronts the environment.

Some topical units might include:

I Food from the Land
    arable lands
    grazing lands
    soils
    pasture lands
    forest lands
    sources of food
            productivity
            methods of harvesting and storage
            processing and distributing
            consumer acceptance

Similarly, topical units could be developed for food from the sea, rivers and waters. Water is another example.

II Water
        precipitation
        water tables
        water as power
        estuaries and tides
        fish spawning sites
        drinkable water

Energy Resources could be another curriculum group of topical units under Energy and Matter.

III Energy Resources
        industrial power and waste
        fossil fuels
        natural gas
        solar energy
        nuclear energy

And so on.

Thus, mathematics would be taught to apply measuring and math skills to solve problems generated within the topical units. I believe that this could be done at all age and grade levels beyond early primary. Students could use their local community land resources--their geography if you will--to investigate decisions about land and water use in their community, and then concentrically to expand and deepen their topical units beyond the local purview to the globe.

A constant problem in curriculum design, that of knowledge integration with other sciences and disciplines, here is minimized because the integrated units are what the student begins with. I have observed teachers who have used the thematic approach to teaching, and have spent entire terms exploring with students the topic of power. It is initially harder to sustain motivation, but once discussion becomes more open the mutual exploration become more intellectually satisfying.

Developing a curriculum for minority students will not in itself solve all the problems associated with their education. Many children will still be disadvantaged in schooling in ways other than cultural adaptation. Nor should the approach to minority curriculum development be a patronizing attempt to mollify minority parents. If schooling is to be a world-encompassing preparation for the real world for children and youth, the development of units in selected minority cultures should be progressing regardless of the school's population composition.

Chapter Six

A CURRICULUM FOR THE MILDLY RETARDED
OF SECONDARY SCHOOL AGE

One of the more persistent problems of educating special education students is the precision of the terms which define their deviation from the norm. Standardized tests of ability, aptitude and skill, together with anecdotal material and interviews, are the main evidence for decisions about placement. Although some kind of labeling seems essential in working with groups of students in need of special remedial attention, the categorizing of students merely by intelligence levels is a dubious distinction. There is a growing uneasiness about intelligence labels, and perhaps even some unfairness in schooling for those defined as retarded.

The general term is "mentally handicapped." This chapter outlines a curriculum model for a specific category within that group--mildly retarded, loosely defined by an I.Q. test score of about 75-90, or in the range of 10-25 points below the average I.Q. test score. In a descending order are the moderately retarded, and the severely retarded. The mildly retarded have also been classified as "educable mentally retarded," to distinguish them from the "trainable mentally retarded," those whose mental handicap is more pronounced.

IDENTIFYING STUDENTS WITH SPECIAL NEEDS

Identifying children and youth who are different mentally, and thus in need of special schooling services, relates in part to how they are identified as different. Much of the problem of identification begins with the testing program.

When Alfred Binet at the turn of the 20th century in Paris attempted to help define the mental and emotional illnesses of those confined to mental institutions he was trying to verify by quantification terms such as "idiot," "moron," and "nincompoop." Binet was looking for an empirical measure for behaviors, and a more adequate diagnostic tool. More current tests measure verbal reasoning (not just vocabulary), arithmetic operations, concepts, spatial orientation, mechanical reasoning, and clerical speed and accuracy.

The Scholastic Aptitude Test (SAT) used for a guide for admissions to higher education in the U.S. is not directly related to a specific curriculum, nor does it measure something called intelligence. It purports to measure aptitude for further academic effort. But descriptive tests, like the Wechsler Scale, do attempt to relate intelligence to a person's total functional ability. The Wechsler Scale operates under the asumption that anyone can perform satisfactorily with enough information. It has a

64

verbal and performance section.

Tests are the principal sources of information about children who need special assistance, and usually act as agents for placement in schooling. Having decided that students need special help, however, the school is now under some obligation to provide the best possible environment to accommodate those differnces. In the U.S., The Education for All Handicapped Children Act mandates a "least restricted environment," and compels schools to develop individual curriculum units for all such identified students.

Intelligence tests, however administered, are only a convenient way of expressing scores on a developed test, relative to the age of the test taker. They are only moderately predictive, not expressive of a permanent state of development, and scores can vary widely over time and circumstances. An I.Q. test does not specify whether or not the behavioral characteristics are attributable to genetic or environmental influences.

Unfortunately, schools have also used testing programs as a means of racially discriminating students. In the U.S. the federal courts have intervened to end this insidious practice, and to correct unacceptable placement programs that segregated students.

There is no long historical tradition for educating the mentally handicapped. Until recent years, the way to deal with the mentally handicapped was to keep them at home if they were not institutionalized. With heightened social awareness and a more humane and egalitarian approach to handicaps, and a greater understanding of the complex biology that results in impairments, educators are the first to deal with the mentally handicapped. Through social pressure, and parental understanding of educational rights, and legislation protecting opportunities to an education, the mentally handicapped have arrived at the school doors for admission.

Most students can eventually learn the most important schooling objectives, given sufficient time, attention, and opportunity. However, many teachers do not want to teach students who are mentally unable or unprepared or in need of extra tutorial assistance. Whether to place the students with the regular classes or to provide special classes for their instruction will be a longstanding debate. In practice, some combination of mainstreaming and special services will benefit best the students defined as retarded.

The ratios vary, but in the U.S. the learning disabled account for about 12 to 15 percent of the schooling population. Many of these students will also be physically handicapped and perhaps have a speech defect. But besides the obvious physical handicaps of vision, hearing, speech and emotional instability, there are many students who are simply below the average in ability and mental capacity. They are not mentally ill, nor necesssarily emotionally disturbed. But in their biological and mental development they may be slower than others at earlier stages of growth. The source of their mental handicap will vary from a genetic defect, a deprived early environment, a childhood disease, or an accident. The medical determination may in fact be very helpful to the school's treatment and placement of the mentally handicapped student.

Mild retardation is only a problem when students who are classified as learning disabled are compared with others of normal ability. The social stigma of their classification as less able can contaminate whatever progress occurs in mental development naturally or through instructional services. The special needs of the mildly retarded are thus often associated with their adjustment to the expectations of their teachers.

The schooling needs of the mildly retarded take on a special dimension because their disability in learning is often recognized when they are forming a psychological concept of themselves. Thus, educators who work with students who have special learning needs should stress attitudinal development for continued normal growth, and not have students lower their expectations for performance in later life.

The response of the school is most often to decide on placement within the schooling context, instead of modifying the school's environment to meet the double disadvantage of students having a learning disability and of coping with adolescent identity. However, there has been recently heightened social awareness of the particular problems of the learning disabled, and students in special need have been identified earlier. Of critical concern are the necessity for special curricular programs and imaginative instructional techniques demanded of educators for such students.

The most important schooling goal for the mildly retarded, in my judgment, is gainful employment. Their hope, and the school's expectation for them, is to find work when finished with secondary schooling. Consequently, the focus of this chapter is to present a sample curriculum for developing a meaningful unit on vocational secondary preparation.

CURRICULUM PROGRAM DEVELOPMENT ISSUES

This sample curriculum assumes that students have been defined as learning disabled, that special teachers have been assigned to work with them and that what is lacking is a curriculum package. The principal issues to be resolved are the curriculum goals and objectives, student objectives for progress, instructional activities, the kind of personnel needed, and the logistics and resources. The primary goal of this kind of program is to prepare such students for employment. The idea is to place graduated students in jobs, and the curriculum becomes the vehicle for developing a comprehensive work-oriented training program.

From my experience in developing such curricula in large school systems, preparatory activities have been grouped around four fields: construction and trades, business practices, public service, and personal services. For example, at the end of a student's participation in a curriculum developing competence in personal services, that student would have demonstrated performance in:

* ability to be interviewed and hired for a job
* ability to relate responsibly with co-workers by
  initiating and carrying on conversations, including
  with friends and strangers
* ability to request help from supervisors
* ability to resolve disputes, both real and probable,
  with co-workers, family members and supervisors

The development of all curriculum units are presumed to relate directly to employment and job performance.

Many of these goals relate purposefully to social skills on the job, an often neglected area of schooling and of curriculum. But such objectives are particularly relevant for the learning disabled and mildly retarded, as their behavior often deviates from the socially acceptable. Special units need to emphasize this part of their schooling performance and preparation for life skills. For example, a module of training emphasizes simulations for job interviews of differing kinds, conducted in an interview room, in which sessions can be video-taped and replayed for analysis. Other units stress potential work-related conflicts between workers and supervisors. Discussion groups help resolve these simulated

PROGRAM GOALS AND OBJECTIVES LESSONS

To develop a program of specific occupational clusters that will enable the student to become employed, remain employed, and get promoted.

OBJECTIVES	CURRICULUM	INSTRUCTION	PERSONNEL	LOGISTICS
To identify or develop a cluster of skills which will increase the student's knowledge and practice of personal work habits, such as honesty, dependability, etc.	To coordinate pre-occupational and iden-tified skills clusters with the new program design.	To arrange visits to occupational centers of major employers.	To coordinate team planning and teaching sessions.	To schedule more time around occupational skill development during regular class sessions.
To identify or develop a cluster of skills which will improve the student's relationships with fellow workers, supervisors, customers and subordinates, such as appearance and attire, respect for others, preferences, etc.	To discuss with business leaders areas of occupational curriculum development.	To organize small group discussion and study sessions for focus on worker plans for social security, benefits, retirement, health, vacations and pensions.	To encourage principals to become more knowledgeable about occupational skill development.	To establish a student sponsored store within the school which buys, sells, advertises and grows in sales.
To identify or develop a cluster of skills which will help the student find a job, keep a job and get promoted.	To identify pre-packaged curricula focusing on occupational skill development.	To participate in role playing sessions which focus on interviewing, recruiting, retention and promotion policies.	To promote staff development exercises among classroom teachers about occupational skill development.	To encourage the use of alternate space during regular school hours for occupational skill development.
	To reassess the present curriculum for possible refinements for occupational development.	To arrange for team teaching sessions on occupational cluster components.		To experiment with shared time and space with local employers and businesses.
	To establish an occupation center where the student learns financing, advertising, buying, selling and merchandizing.	To arrange for business and labor leaders and union organizers to speak to students.		To petition for community transportation for special services.

exercises and permit students to experience what is expected of them on the job.

PROGRAM GOALS

Curriculum development teams can identify multiple goals for programs for the learning disabled, but I believe that there are four worth special consideration. They are:

> 1. To improve communication skills, especially the
>   basic skills of reading and writing, listening and
>   speaking and quantitative reasoning, as a result of
>   student interest in a specific vocational area.

After exploration of several possible employment areas, students will choose a particular one for mastery at their ability level. The overall schooling goal is vocational: not for students merely to complete schooling, but to prepare them for specific employment.

> 2. To develop a program based on individual student
>   aptitude and vocational interest within four major
>   vocational areas: business practices, construction
>   and trades, public services, and personal services.

The identification of individual aptitude and ability is just as important among the mildly retarded as it is among students of mixed ability levels. I suggest that vocational interest inventories be administered to such students to determine their vocational inclinations. It is difficult to actually visit a wide number of employment sites, but as far as possible this is highly desirable. Small discussion groups can increase student awareness of specific employment areas, and laboratory sessions can be practice areas for the improvement of skills necessary for obtaining jobs within a chosen industry.

> 3. To develop personal and social attitudes and
>   competencies essential for successful living at
>   home, in school, in the community, and on the job.

This goal presumes that there are curriculum units on personal habits, such as sound health and nutritional standards, good grooming practices, and acceptable attitudes toward self and work. The purpose here is also to develop in the special student social attitudes of how to relate to others, and respect for the rights and privileges of others. Included in specific student objectives are the development of home-making skills, and child-rearing practices.

For employment purposes, the curriculum units will also stress punctuality, dependablity, initiative, cooperation, and acceptance of the consequences for personal action and behavior. Students who have low mental abilities are usually unable to recognize the thresholds of powerful emotions as they arise, and are often prone to wild and frenetic behavior disturbing to those who don't understand or sympathize, like prospective employers. This occurs when they are frustrated or mildly angry or unable to perform satisfactorily. Social skill development, quite intense, should be an integral of the curriculum program for such students.

SURVEY FORM--CURRICULUM FOR MILDLY RETARDED

	PERCEPTION ABOUT CONCEPT				PERCEPTION ABOUT IMPLEMENTATION			
	Essential	Important	Somewhat Important	Not Important	Very Probable	Somewhat Probable	Possible to do	Impossible to do
11. Our schools need to disseminate research findings about problems of the mildly retarded to all teachers involved with the project.								
12. The personalities of the teachers involved with the mildly retarded are critical factors in the success of the program.								
13. Each participating school needs to revise and adapt the time schedules to meet the special needs of the mildly retarded.								
14. Each school needs to modify the instructional techniques to adapt to the special needs of the mildly retarded.								
15. Each school needs to establish a formal and informal communication network to report on progress.								
16. Special teachers and regular classroom teachers should be held accountable for both successes and problems.								
17. Each mildly retarded youth should have continuous diagnostic surveys to determine progress.								
18. Every effort should be made to bring community and business and labor leaders into the program's operations.								
19. The present academic curriculum ought to be redirected into the proposed vocationally-oriented curriculum for the mildly retarded youth.								
20. Parents should play a large role in the formulation of the program plans and their eventual implementation.								

SURVEY FORM--CURRICULUM FOR MILDLY RETARDED

DIRECTIONS: Please place a check mark in the appropriate spaces for each of the two sections, Perception about the Concept (as expressed by the statement) and in the section headed Perception about Implementation, which best expresses whether or not you feel the concept could ever work in your school.

	PERCEPTION ABOUT CONCEPT				PERCEPTION ABOUT IMPLEMENTATION			
	Essential	Important	Somewhat Important	Not Important	Very Probable	Somewhat Probable	Possible to do	Impossible to do
1. Occupational skill development for the mildly retarded of intermediate and high school age is essential for their later success.								
2. Mildly retarded children of this age level need special attention from teachers.								
3. Mildly retarded children should receive special support services other children do not.								
4. A special effort needs to be made to insure the placement of these children and youth in jobs for which they have been specially trained by the school.								
5. Vocational education teachers should have some major responsibilities for the development and implementation of a program in occupational skills.								
6. This kind of a program should be largely developed by all the participants in the program.								
7. Principals should assume the responsibility for the overall logistics, including time, space and resource allocation.								
8. Counselors need to participate in this program.								
9. Career counseling is an integral part of the effort in job placement.								
10. Coordinators should assume the major responsibility for overall coordination of resources, scheduling and room arrangements.								

4. To develop a curriculum program of specific occupational clusters that will enable the student to
become employed, remain employed and get promoted.

Although there will be many areas of overlap in the curriculum that
prepares mildly retarded students for occupations, there will be specific
differences between skills in construction and trades and, for example,
skills in clerical services training. Units early in the program will allow
students to explore a full range of occupations, then to choose an area of
training, and finally to develop increased competencies necessary for
specific employment in a designated job. I have included a sample set of
considerations according to program units for the development of the
particular goal.

SURVEY QUESTIONAIRE FORM

The sample survey form included here can be used to gather
information about a curriculum program for students with special needs,
and to obtain evidence about possible consensus on goals and objectives. It
can be used with teachers, administrators, parents, or community
representatives. It is not a survey of attitudes, values or beliefs. It only
attempts to measure whether or not people tend to agree with the basic
principles of the program. It is wise to seek some degree of consensus about
the goals of a curriculum program prior to further development. If there is
significant disagreement, then it would be politic to revise the program
goals. The first objective is to discover how the intended public perceives
the goals, and secondly how they think such a program would work in
their school.

CONCLUSION

Only in recent memory have handicapped children and youth entered
schools, partly as a result of increased social pressure and partly from
active legislation, particularly in the U.S. The Education for All
Handicapped Children Act. The body of litigation on behalf of the
handicapped is growing and is defining and protecting in greater detail the
rights and privileges of all handicapped children. Educating a
handicapped student is much more costly for schools, and this factor by
itself has limited more extensive school services.

But besides the legal framework, schools still must rely on imperfect
methods for defining handicaps, placing handicapped students in
appropriate programs, and evaluating their progress. Once within a
program, a handicapped student, particularly a mildly retarded student
who can benefit from a supportive schooling environment, needs a defined
curriculum. Such a curriculum model as I have suggested here, developed
for the 13th largest school system in the U.S., Fairfax County schools in
northern Virginia, can assist educators in improving the content and
delivery of services for this special population.

Chapter Seven

A SAMPLE CURRICULUM FOR THE
PHYSICALLY HANDICAPPED STUDENT

Because the physically handicapped are also often learning disabled, the specialized teacher must not only confront the lack of normal mobility in the child, but also the mild to severe impairments towards normal skill achievement. Common symptoms of both disabilities thus combine to make the teaching task an exercise in extraordinary patience. Some symptoms include hyperactivity--most often associated with learning disabilities--impulsivity, the lack of attending behavior, and the like.

Learning disabled children who are also physically handicapped *can* learn, but not necessarily in the same way or with the same techniques that the teacher uses with other children or youth. Classifying children as either learning disabled or physically handicapped, however, does not ease either teacher diagnosis or prescription. The individualization of instruction is as appropriate to each of their unique cases as it is to other students. The teacher, whose instructional acts are the curriculum, sharpens the appropriateness of the activities by means of well-planned and designed outlines for teaching action.

The purpose of this chapter is to describe some ways in which development activities and training exercises might be useful in preparing a program for the physically handicapped child or youth.

Designing curriculum packages for the physically handicapped is usually regarded as a curse by teachers, therapists and aides, shouldered into service for that purpose. Where to begin? For educators not trained in curriculum development, the process of what to do first in designing a comprehensive curriculum for a particular group of special children is a difficult one. Those initial frustrations can be reduced with sample outlines for curriculum design which I propose here.

PLANNING SEQUENCES AND GENERAL GOAL DEVELOPMENT

What is important to establish first is a sequence of planning activities that will reduce unnecessary discussion and work duplication among the curriculum committee members. Central to this sequence is the agreement on the broad goals for a handicapped student upon completion of secondary schooling. Notice that the goal development specifies the ultimate criterion, *completion of high school*, and not the process goal of what to do during schooling. The following goals were agreed upon and adopted into use by a large (130,000 plus students) suburban school system.

Upon completion of secondary schooling, the student will be able to:

1. demonstrate communication skills basic to the development of other learning;
2. have a realistic awareness of his or her handicap;
3. have a knowledge of individual and group leisure time and recreational activities;
4. demonstrate behavior appropriate in interpersonal relationships;
5. exhibit and cope with changes associate with physical, social and emotional development;
6. discriminate values and establish value systems, and learn to respect the values of others and their opinions;
7. make decisions and accept the responsibilities and consequences for those decisions;
8. demonstrate the skills necessary with getting and keeping a job;
9. demonstrate the functional skills associated with everyday living;
10. demonstrate a knowledge and understanding of the basic academic skills appropriate to his or her developmental capacities and those of general education.

Let me make a few points about these goals. First, you will note that all are student-oriented, not teacher, school and subject-matter oriented. Second, that with the exception of the last objective, which includes all those understandings we normally have about curriculum and what it is, the goals are practically oriented to what the student needs to complete school. Incorporated in the goals is the recognition of the child's handicap. Third, implicit in the goal development is the recognition that the activities must be built around the student, not just adjusted to fit already existing plans.

DETERMINING SKILL LEVELS

A second step in curriculum planning development is to determine the differing levels of student behavior for sequencing. Level I may be described as the beginning level of functional development for handicapped students with minimal skills. Level II could be an intermediate stage for students with some skill in a particular goal, who need extra guidance, support and curriculum adaptations. Level III could be appropriate to those handicapped students who are becoming more proficient and need less assistance and adaptation.

These levels of development are not to be confused with mental or chronological ages, though each clearly has a bearing on the student's development. Young handicapped students would generally start at Level I in a curriculum scheme, but older students with mental or constraining physical disabilities may also be functioning at Level I. Because of the wide variability in mental and physical disabilities, some students will only be able to achieve Level I of the goals in many areas, but every student's program should include all goals at the appropriate level. A diagnostic profile will assist in planning each student's individual program incorporating the appropriate levels. Some older students may have individual programs at all levels when certain motor or mental abilities express themselves in developmental lag.

Together with each curricular level should go a definiton of terms used in the explanation of each goal and all the sequencing of specific objectives which follow. These definitions will help standardize working phrases useful for parent conferences and for general education dissemination among other school programs.

DEVELOPING SPECIFIC BEHAVIORAL OBJECIVES

The development of specific student objectives constitutes the third step. For example, under Goal 2--"The student will be able to have a realistic awareness of his or her own handicap"--several curriculum objectives, expressed in terminal student behavior can be developed. Thus, a sequence of student behavioral objectives for this goal could be similar to the following (see also the tables for further elaboration):

The student will be able to:
1. define the handicap (such as cerebral palsy, its causes and prognosis);
2. demonstrate acceptance of the disability and know its limitations and capabilities;
3. learn to recognize prejudgment and to deal with these attitudes in others and himself or herself;
4. be able to identify and use adaptive devices appropriate to his or her handicap;
5. be able to maintain his or her devices;
6. demonstrate personal habits that pertain to personal and medical health.

These specific student behavioral objectives are thus a part of the general goal of making the student aware of his or her particular handicap, so essential to present and future human relationships and basic to the rest of functional learning. The student must understand how he or she is impaired, and how to live and function successfully with that impairment. All of these objectives would be a part of Level I attainment, and therefore applicable to all.

Here are some sample objectives taken from a few of the general development goals (consult again the table for details):

1. Objectives from the general goal on individual and group recreational activities: demonstrate mental games one can play alone; select an interest area from among hobbies; participate in at least one community sponsored program.

2. Objectives from the general goal in interpersonal relationships: be able to greet family members, friends, and strangers; use normal expressions of language and expression appropriate to the handicap; use different bodily postures and eating habits.

3. Objectives from the general goal associated with physical, social and emotional development: identify major and gross emotional expressions such as fear, anger, happiness, etc; identify different family members, and social and emotional interactions within a family unit; identify other places for living (camps, communes, hospital, kibbutz, etc.)

GOAL -- TO COPE WITH CHANGES, ASSOCIATED WITH PHYSICAL, SOCIAL, AND EMOTIONAL DEVELOPMENT -- LEVEL I

INSTRUCTION	RESOURCES	LOGISTICS
The teacher will-		
- provide for the demonstration of live and simulated expressions of major emotions, facial and bodily.	puppets, role playing, pictures, films	
- provide for the demonstration and simulation of major states of conscious behavior, such as withdrawal, isolation, etc.	professional associations, films, community service agencies	
- use photographs of child's own family and other family pictures.	pictures, wooden people, real people, Peabody Kit, photographs	family day, camera, permission for photographs
- provide time for 1) dress up as family members, 2) dramatize family roles (role playing, puppets), 3) art.	puppets, clothes, dolls, house keeping, art supplies, workshop, tape records.	workshop with family, counselor
- use films, stories, field trips to show child activities a family could enjoy.	films, stories	field trips, picnics
- use pictures, discussion, stories, to identify various places a child could live, other than a family unit--role play interaction in these situations.	puppets, pictures, films, hospital	field trips to hospital

GOAL -- REALISTIC AWARENESS OF HANDICAP -- LEVEL I

OBJECTIVES	EVALUATION
The student will-	The student will-
-define handicap (such as Cerebral Palsy) (causes, prognosis).	- be able to relate to adults and other children that "I am not contagious," "I was born this way," or "I am not sick."
- demonstrate acceptance of disability and know limitations and capabilities.	- in a simulated situation be able to express limitations and know when to ask for help.
- learn to recognize prejudgment and learn to deal with these attitudes in others and in self.	- acknowledge and distinguish physical tasks he can and cannot do.
- be able to identify and use adaptive devices and procedures appropriate to handicap.	- indicate which devices are useful for different tasks, e.g., mobility and communication devices.
- be able to maintain devices.	- demonstrate the proper care and maintenance, such as use, storage, cleaning, repair.
- demonstrate personal habits that pertain to medical and personal health.	- be able to demonstrate to teachers and parents appropriate habits of personal hygiene, body cleanliness, restroom needs.

N.B. Level I is the level of lowest ability and performance.

GOAL -- REALISTIC AWARENESS OF HANDICAP -- LEVEL I

INSTRUCTION	RESOURCES	LOGISTICS

The teacher will-

- use 1) pictures of the student and other babies with the student's handicap, 2) puppets, 3) role playing exercises.	Films on Cerebral Palsy, puppets, felt boards, pictures.	Trips to humane shelters, clinics, botanical gardens, woods and parks.
- engage children in motor tasks such as jumping, drawing, running, sewing, pouring, stirring, etc.	Cards, cups, jump ropes, crayons, pens.	
- demonstrate the use of devices appropriate to specific needs of handicap.	mannikins, films, handicapped people, commercial firms, all available devices.	Go to commercial firms, clinics.
- demonstrate the proper care, maintenance, repair, cleaning and use of each device.		
- demonstrate with the child how to go to the restroom, bathe, wash hands, comb hair, change diapers, brush teeth, and use special devices.	brushes, combs, towels, films, soap, posters, charts, dolls, puppets.	trip to restroom, refrigerator, pill dispenser.

GOAL -- TO COPE WITH CHANGES, ASSOCIATED WITH
PHYSICAL, SOCIAL, AND EMOTIONAL DEVELOPMENT -- LEVEL I

OBJECTIVES	EVALUATION
The student will-	The student will-
- identify in self major and gross emotional expressions such as fear, anger, happiness, sadness, loneliness, crisis in self.	- demonstrate facial expressions and bodily postures associated with major expressive emotions.
- identify social/emotional changes in others.	N/A at Level I (but at other Ability Levels)
- identify physical changes by distinguishing waking from sleeping, fantasy and imaginative states from concrete reality.	- simulate behaviors associated with major states of fantasy and attending behavior.
- identify members of immediate family unit (mother, father, siblings and other family units).	- indicate members of immediate family by use of photographs and put together pictures to complete a family unit.
- identify basic social and emotional interactions within a family group.	- demonstrate various family roles by acting or use of dolls.
- identify activities for family interaction.	- indicate (list or point) activities he would like to have his family do together.
- identify other places for living, i.e., hospital, kibbutz, half-way homes, group homes, and groups.	- indicate other places of living than in a home by telling or pointing to pictures.

The sixth and seventh goals have to do with social and attitudinal development...curricular units sometimes omitted because of the difficulty in constructing them. Clearly, the student needs a wide variety of learning experiences in order to establish a personal value system. It seems that one of the concerns of teachers of the physically handicapped is to assist the student in knowing and selecting values he or she can live by. The value system itself is not to be considered permanent and inflexible, but will change with time, knowledge, and experience. Part of the teacher's role would be to introduce alternatives from which the student can re-assess choices and decisions. A supportive atmosphere will help create a climate of respect and empathy.

The problems of mobility, dialogue, and behavior are frequently more complex than in non-handicapped children. If the child or youth is to move and communicate, many specialists will have to provide structured conditions for student choice. A suggested sequence for helping fulfill the general goal of making decisions and accepting the responsibility for their consequences is recognition of a problem, consideration of probable solutions, deciding on a course of action, acting on that decision, and accepting the flow that results from that decision. The sequence sounds easy, but teaching the rationale and sequence itself to children whose movement, dialogue and behavior are seriously impaired requires unbelievable patience, skill, and perserverance.

Consequently, one objective under the general goal about decision-making would be for the student to recognize and anticipate the consequences of his or her movement, behavior and dialogue. Each teacher can stimulate and reinforce situations that provide students with choices about their actions for retrieving, removing or avoiding objects or people, curbing abusive dialogue and errant behavior.

But in the long run, even more important to successful coping with the world of the physically able, the handicapped child or youth needs to develop self-sufficiency that leads to employment. The root and core of the curriculum efforts must lead to skills needed for getting and keeping a job. The development of a positive self-image, appropriate social skills, and task-specific skills are part of the curriculum sequence. Specific objectives would thus have to do with time and punctuality, etiquette, dress and appearance, personal hygiene, respect for authority, good work attitudes and the like.

Nor can the curriculum neglect those tasks which develop the functional skills needed for daily living. Those movements, standard modes of behavior, and conditioned reflexes easily accomplished by the non-handicapped cannot be presumed for the physically disabled. Common modes of dress, proper eating habits, basic foods, negotiating around obstacles (elevators, narrow doorways, curbs, revolving doors, escalators, etc.) the identification of transportation, standard home appliances and their operation, simple recipes, functional cleaning devices and their use, minor repairs around an apartment or home--all of these conditions need to be a significant part of the planned objectives and conscious teaching effort. They cannot be assumed as known or understood.

The object is to allow the handicapped youth the opportunity to become mostly independent in normal living conditions. This can only be done through a conscious identification and teaching of those tasks critical to independent living.

IDENTIFYING TEACHING STRATEGIES, RESOURCES , LOGISTICS

Once general development goals and their specific behavioral objectives have been agreed upon and written, the fourth step is to specify those particular teaching strategies, resources and logistic concerns that will materially assist in fulfilling those objectives for each student. Let's take an example from the general goal of functional skill development for everyday living.

Student Learning Objective	Teaching Strategy	Resources	Logistics
The student will be able to use or ask for help when confronted with a structural barrier	The teacher will confront the student with barriers and instruct him or her in the best means of negotiating them	Public buildings, ramps, curbs, car entries	Time and accessibility to places outside the school, busy sidewalks, interiors of buildings

The proper evaluation of the success in satisfying this objective is if the student can negotiate the barrier by the best means at his or her disposal; if not, then to seek nearby assistance from friends or strangers.

If this comprehensive curriculum is developed by a committee then the next step is to acquaint the rest of the faculty and staff with the developed design. This brings us to the fifth and last step which is to design a series of training exercises for appropriate personnel.

SAMPLE TRAINING EXERCISES

A one to three day workshop can be organized to help familiarize personnel who did not participate in the curriculum development, and to further clarify the teaching problems for those who did help develop the curriculum.

One method for opening workshop participation is to check the level of agreement about the central purposes. Each general goal can be stated and participants can check their beliefs about its inclusion in the project and their perception about whether or not it will work. A sample check list might look like that in the accompanying diagram.

A review of the goals and general assumptions underlying the curriculum and degrees of agreement about them will provide an engaging discussion for a workshop opening.

ROLE PLAYING SIMULATIONS

A simulation is a training exercise under controlled conditions. The playing of a role usually involves the player exposing perceptions about how a person would act, and dialogue a person might say in a specified situation. The advantages of the role playing simulation are: 1) exposing differing perceptions about a mutual problem; 2) assuming another's viewpoint and perspective; and 3) discussing the differences in views and roles.

The role playing format in this kind of a training exercise for

SURVEY FORM–CURRICULUM FOR MILDLY RETARDED

DIRECTIONS: Please place a check mark in the appropriate spaces for each of the two sections, Perception about the Concept (as expressed by the statement) and in the section headed Perception about Implementation, which best expresses whether or not you feel the concept could ever work in your school.

1. The curriculum for PH should be developmental, that is related to the individual growth rate and pacing of each student.

2. A part of this curriculum should focus on social, manipulative and inter-personal skills as well as cognitive ones.

3. etc.

	PERCEPTION ABOUT CONCEPT				PERCEPTION ABOUT IMPLEMENTATION			
	Essential	Important	Somewhat Important	Not Important	Very Probable	Somewhat Probable	Possible to do	Impossible to do
1.								
2.								
3.								

personnel working with the physically handicapped reduces the time for planning more briefly. It compresses what might typically involve interactions with large numbers into a brief time span. The main idea is for the personnel involved in both the development and implementation of the curriculum to share their ideas in a productive way and abbreviated time frame.

The immediate purpose is to give workshop participants by means of simulations some practical suggestions for improving the program. What will emerge from these exercises will be information gaps in those who play roles other than their own or those they are familiar with.

A sample simulation exercise can be developed for both elementary and secondary personnel. Let's take a look at a sample simulation for secondary.

> The problem is with John. His profile is that he is sixteen years old, of low normal intelligence, has spastic cerebral palsy, a low level of motivation, poor proficiency in basic motor skills, inappropriate social behavior, and the prognosis is that he needs to continue in therapy and seems to have no reinforcement or follow-through from his parents.
>
> John's employer, who is willing to hire handicapped youth in his fast food business, is about to fire John because he is becoming a nuisance to his work group. He is periodically late, his appearance and hygiene are poor, and he is occasionally obnoxious to fellow workers. The employer readily admits, however, that when John does work, he does it well.
>
> A conference is called in the principal's office. Present are the employer (or designate), the principal, the team leader for Physically Handicapped (P.H.), an aide, a teacher of the P.H. and a regular classroom teacher who has a few P.H. youth.
>
> The team leader feels John is working at the wrong job. The regular classroom teacher feels John has got to be pulled out of the work situation and drilled in the academics. The aide believes John needs the working situation but needs further training in social and interpersonal skills.
>
> Help resolve the issue to John's best advantage.

The time participants are allowed to digest, discuss and report on progress may vary. One aspect will surely emerge: there is no set pattern for solution of a common problem. But the role playing simulation--and roles can be varied within the group or rotated--serves to highlight where pattern of divergence might occur and how to prevent differences among faculty and staff that can/will lead to serious misunderstanding and disagreement later.

These sample curricular plans and training exercises can be modified for specific audiences, such as parent groups or principals.

Beginning the development of a comprehensive curriculum for physically handicapped children and youth requires an active leadership endorsement. Full participation from among selected teachers, aides and supervisors is also essential. The training workshops can give definite clarity to ill-perceived or misunderstood issues among all levels of personnel. Ultimately, however, all the designs, simulated dilemmas and exercises will fail unless there is general consensus of purpose and direction, and a uniform commitment to achieve the proposed aims.

Chapter Eight

AN ALTERNATIVE PROGRAM FOR DISRUPTIVE STUDENTS

What's the best way to handle adolescent students with moderate to severe behavioral problems? Students who consistently disrupt normal classrooms are a thorn to any teacher. Their disruptive behavior is a manifestation, a consequence of multiple causes, mostly attributable to poor home or community life. The causes may include a negligent home environment, a learning disability, poor reading skills, a disrespect or disregard for authority (or self), and so on. In the rural northeastern community in which I developed the program in this chapter, we found that students with the most nagging behavior problems came from one parent families where there was little respect for the value of education, and where the discipline of the child was either nonexistent or excessively cruel.

Often, schools find that the most expeditious way to reduce such disruptive students in regular classrooms is to set them apart in an alternative program, to isolate their behavior.

Students who create disturbances are sometimes too easily classified as a discipline problem when a wide variety of learning problems, emotional disturbances, or skill weaknesses may be the source of their disruptive behavior. Fighting, yelling, lying, stealing, personal insults, and breaking equipment characterize some of these students' behavior, and it creates tremendous difficulties for a regular classroom teacher who often cannot cope with one or more students who habitually disrupt classes.

Separate instructional programs designed for such students balances the need to preserve some tranquillity in regular classes, while creating a special, alternative program for students who are identified as disruptive but not necessarily in need of special education services. Isolating such students may create more instructional and learning difficulties than a program hopes to solve. As a stopgap measure, however, it is one way for secondary administrators to plan appropriate instructional strategies for a growing adolescent group.

Let me outline some of the steps in such a program design.

THE NEED FOR ASSESSING DISRUPTIVE STUDENTS

Before preparing suitable program objectives, it is necessary to determine precise criteria for admitting students into the program. This includes, minimally, data on the physical, psychological, attitudinal, aptitude and interest, achievement levels and capabilities of likely candidates for the program.

Information on what conditions set disruptive children apart from the children in regular classsrooms is crucial to program success. From a student's perspective, it could be disastrous for a particular child to be erroneously misplaced and mislabeled. The judgment of school officials needs to be clear and unequivocable by precisely defining what kind of disruptive behavior needs special instructional and curricular alternatives. The needs assessment provides such critical baseline data.

Moreover, no clear program objectives can be defined with accuracy without this information. Students who have been referred and admitted into the program based on insufficient evidence could be injuriously discriminated against by faulty teacher perceptions.

EXAMPLES OF DIAGNOSIS

The first step in diagnosing candidates for an alternative program for disruptive students is to establish a comprehensive battery of tests to determine whether or not a student should be referred to the program. Standardized tests are already available in physical health, basic skills and achievement levels. Examples of items on a physical health check list might include:

1. Physical Health
   general health status
   vision
   hearing
   dental
   innoculation history
   urinalysis
   energy level

2. Mental Health
   personal relations
   peer activities
   mental health record
   counseling history

3. Nutrition
   knowledge of nutrition standards
   daily nutrition needs
   hygienic behavior

4. Social Services
   employment concerns and ambitions
   community agency support
   etc.

Teachers associated with the program ought to participate in the development of other easily administered forms that reveal information about a disruptive student's affective development. An example of such a check list might look like that in the accompanying diagram.

It could be administered to the students who are candidates for entry into an alternative program; or school officials could test teacher perceptions of selected students. The information will be used to determine how a student is admitted into the program, and how he or she gets out.

Summarized Affective Development Needs for _____
(Name)

	Very Positive	Positive	Negative	Very Negative
Attitude				
towards self				
towards school				
towards home				
towards learning				
Motivation and Aspiration				
towards the need to achieve				
towards expressed interests				
towards chosen occupations				
Temperament				
towards being alone				
towards relying on others				
towards hostility				
Interpersonal				
towards working with others				
towards accepting advice				
towards making choices				
towards assuming tasks				
towards opposing ideas				

TRAINING TEACHERS ABOUT STUDENT ASSESSMENT

The second step in the needs assessment, after gathering information useful to determining the student's entry into the program, is to illustrate for teachers in regular classrooms how to recommend students for testing, or even administer tests for students themselves. The third step is to train all participating teachers, regular classroom personnel and those who will teach in the alternative program, in proper evaluation techniques of disruptive student behavior, and systematic use of such instruments for the program.

The results of a comprehensive analysis of a disruptive student's needs will help identify the probable cause of disruptive behavior. As a result, teachers can plan improved instructional units for eliminating such behavior. Such information will, moreover, permit an improved analysis of children's abilities and deficiencies in regular classrooms, and enable participating teachers to become more aware of the complexity involved in judging disruptive students.

The reason for insisting on an accurate and complete data system should be clear: instructional objectives developed on the basis of more complete student information will more likely be successfully achieved than objectives developed with imprecise student information.

DEVELOPMENT OF OBJECTIVES

Once the proper student information needed has been agreed upon and administered, and criteria for program *entrance* and *exit* behaviors established, those objectives most appropriate for disruptive students need development. These should include the development of curricular objectives that allow students to recognize and eliminate specific disruptive behaviors that are habitual, such as withdrawing, stealing, hitting, swearing, personally insulting remarks and so on. These will likely often be accompanied by reading and communication skills difficulties.

A part of the objective, besides noting the disruptive symptom, should attempt to define what the student is expected to do in a positive manner. The objective should not read like a commandment, "Thou shalt not steal," but state what specific activities will reduce or eliminate stealing, like those which develop respect for property.

Thus, the objective might be: "Students who have been known to steal frequently will participate in reading and other activities that deal with respect for property." The accompanying instructional strategies will allow teachers to organize reading matter around larceny cases, petty thievery and recent local court cases in theft. Students could attend court cases on such topics. The idea is to blend the development of basic skills, such as reading around topics of interest that build student acknowledgement of their disruptive behavior.

SAMPLE OBJECTIVES

Other examples of curricular objectives for such an alternate program for disruptive students might include the following:

> Students who exhibit withdrawal (non-participatory) behavior will participate in study groups and will practice listening and reporting skills.

Students who consistently exhibit forceful hitting behavior (for reasons not known to the teacher) will be exposed to non-violent ways of solving problems by tutoring handicapped children, attending court on assault and battery charges, studying mental health cases, speaking with victims of assault crimes, etc.

Students who swear indiscriminately will replace offensive words with agreeable ones by identifying and using acceptable substitutes.

Children who show destructive behavior such as excessive littering, knife-cutting, breaking equipment, etc. will participate in group clean-ups, money-making activities, and purchase of new equipment.

These examples are illustrations of the kinds of objectives that both recognize the presence of disruptive behavior and attempt to reduce or eliminate them.

CASE STUDY

For example, after analyzing "Susie's" results from the diagnostic testing we find that she has average results in the physical, psychological and development components but that her interpersonal skills are deficient and her reading difficulties pronounced. Her traits which got her admitted into the program are: poor reading, lying and personal insults, and occasional stealing. We decide that she does not need professional referral outside the system, and have organized her needs to be: 1) reading; 2) lying behavior correction; 3) stealing behavior correction; and 4) positive reinforcement of group and interpersonal skills development.

Contingent upon advisory committee or selected staff judgment, a number of children exhibit both reading difficulties and lying behavior. These children can be sub-grouped within the Alternative Program for fixed periods of time into instructional units which concentrate on both reading and the extinction of lying behaviors. This can be in the hands of one instructor who teaches to the student objectives in this area exclusively for a fixed period of time, or one or more instructors working in tandem...but always to the agreed-upon objectives.

The important point in organizing and ordering the time and the instructional units and the personnel is that they should be handled simply; that is, with a minimum of interference from each other--one teacher handling one or two objectives for a fixed period of time, all known to the student or students involved.

The second significant issue is that, not only should the instructional organization be simple (exclusively on reading, for example) and known by the students, but it should be evaluated continuously to determine the impact of the concentrated method.

ORGANIZATIONAL SKILLS

The key elements in the program will likely be a) organization of the instruction; b) consistency in following a rational plan; c) time; and d) personnel.

The organization and consistency will hopefully be determined when program goals are established from the analysis of the individual children's needs assessment.

Time structuring, however, might be patterned in the following fashion:

READING

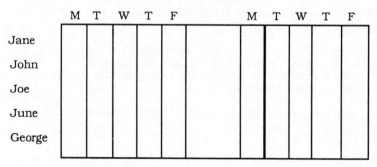

Reading, thus, could be a two-week immersion phase for selected students with known reading difficulties. At the end of the two week assessment towards improvement, these children either exit into another instructional unit--perhaps a group activity to extinguish stealing--or remain for an extended--but again fixed and known period, perhaps one more week--until significant improvement results.

Or children may be *eased* out of the reading unit and gradually phased into another acivity one day of the chosen week then two days, etc.

Personnel assignments must be explicit and accountable. If experts, such as reading specialists are required, then they should be programmed in for specified activities or on a short-term basis. Specific criteria need to be determined for personnel assignments. One example, which again will be culled from an analysis of what is required as a result of the needs inventory of disruptive children, is for one or two full-time instructor(s) who draw on the resource skills of many specialists who work in the program for only short periods.

Again, the nature of the personnel assignments must flow from an establishment of the specific goals and objectives.

CONCLUSION

Lastly, the purpose of the Alternative Education Program should be conducted in the spirit of an inquiry into the investigation of the causes and sources of student disruptive bahavior, and a discovery of the best ways of eliminating disruptive behavior in children--whether in special programs or regular school settings. To this end, it is necessary to experiment broadly with unproven and perhaps untested techniques. The value of this experimental procedure lies in its potential applicability throughout the school system. Consider the value of the discovery of a system which successfully extinguishes fighting behavior. Such a series of techniques, applied by regular classroom teachers, eliminates potential student applicants into the program and enhances the child's staying power in the "mainstream."

But consider also the possible results of never having tried to experiment creatively with alternative methods of extinguishing disruptive behavior. The choice appears obvious.

The Alternative Education Program, once having clearly defined its central purposes and activities, cannot turn back, cannot operate business as usual in the content or form of its instruction. To send a child back to his or her parent school for discipline reinforces in the child's mind that the program and its attendant rewards and punishments is not "alternative" or special at all. It reinforces the concept of tracking and that though perhaps physically removed from other classrooms and children, it is still just another classroom.

In fact, the danger is that because the program will be developing and experimenting with new curricular and instructional methods, some children may want to become admitted for the variety it offers, and do so by feigning disruptive behavior. The irony and paradox of this possibility will demonstrate more convincingly than anything else the need for inculcating quickly into the regular school's program whatever educational benefits results fom the creative and innovative techniques proven useful from the Alternative Program.

No school program can long survive without the support and cooperation of the community and especially the parents of children in a special program. Consistent with that understanding, special efforts should be begun which both solicit parental help and support, and seek specific advice and volunteer help on an *ad hoc* basis. Periodic meetings, social gatherings, telephone surveys and discussions, all manner of formal and informal communication and mutually cooperative links, will help forge new relations between parents and school officials.

Chapter Nine

MANAGING THE CURRICULUM

The school curriculum is like the Mercator Projection on a world map: it has expanded to fill the scales of latitude and longitude from that of a circle to a rectangle. And it has accomplished this illusion without seeming to have changed our perspective of the globe. Like the Mercator Projection, the curriculum has changed the shape of things by distorting the units for measuring reality. But unlike a cartographer, or the inventor of the illogical typewriter key board, it is not easy to rearrange a better system.

The curriculum is subject in a democracy to multiple levels of influences: the state of the economy; the politics of the day; responses by the common culture (and various sub-cultures); the perceived needs of an expanding number of client groups (like vocational education); and professional interests of teachers. All of these interests vie for playing time on the curriculum field.

This chapter is concerned with the management of the curriculum in a few selected areas. I discuss management of the curriculum from a school, not a teacher, perspective.

THE SCHOOL POPULATION AS CURRICULUM MANAGER

The student composition of the school can, in a relative sense, contribute to how the curriculum is managed at both an institutional and instructional level. This is especially true in a multicultural student body. Institutional curriculum managers can ignore student differences, as teachers cannot, and continue to emphasize the pertinence of the knowledge-based curriculum, but only at the expense of wide alienation and disaffection.

Furthermore, advances in electronic media have broadened the base of communication and knowledge, once only gained through schooling, and have made information available to the general public, almost instantaneously. Thus, for many students, knowledge is attainable by means of radio, television, videos and music, and teachers are not necessarily seen as knowledge experts. The curriculum of life is no rival for the schooling curriculum in the minds of many adolescents.

For the few who early in life desire to learn even at the expense of gratification and social life, the school will never have a problem. But there are many who reject altogether the culture of the school. There are also many who never accept what the school has to offer. For the large number of those students who are intellectually under-developed, slow in motivation for learning, antagonistic to un-inspiring teachers, and un-responsive to the subjects taught, managing the currriculum may imply changing the delivery system drastically.

To accommodate students deemed difficult to reach, some schools have re-packaged the curriculum for those who do not want, wouldn't accept, or probably wouldn't succeed in most academic environments. The selection of content has become a primary decision in managing the curriculum. It has become more difficult because curriculum relevance has been based often on this larger sociological dimension: that everyone should receive the rudiments of an education regardless of ability, aptitude or competence. By reducing, if not eliminating, the student drop-out or school-leavers problem, schools are now faced with the many students who are only marginally capable. The price for the satisfaction of equality of educational opportunity is declining test scores, disruptive and disinterested students, and a weakened curriculum.

Given this current social phenomenon, which goes beyond the question of what constitutes a "core" curriculum in a school, it is not surprising that the school must manage the adjustment of content that appeals to all levels of students. The existence of so much content and so many courses, especially in secondary schools, appears to repudiate the existence of a legitimate core of knowledge all need to function in a democratic society. The process of curriculum development seems to add to, never subtract from, the inventory of offerings. Consequently, managing the curriculum often now means developing programs to fit the expanding needs of students who lack requisite academic skills.

Conversely, the needs of the talented and gifted among the student population might also be systematically ignored. Because instruction is normally directed towards the average in ability in the class, students on either end of an ability scale tend to be out of touch. The talented and the gifted will survive well in spite of schooling and ennui. Nevertheless, with sympathetic instruction and an appropriately designed curriculum for the advanced learner, the opportunities can be enhanced and the learning capabilities multiplied at a crucial age in development.

The ideal curriculum incorporates the needs of the society, and benefits from the living structure of the traditional organized base of knowledge. But it also cannot ignore the specific learning needs of the resident student population. Social mobility has brought about rapid population shifts and the school feels the weight of these societal pressures. The learning needs of the student is a paramount component of developing and managing the curriculum.

Students themselves--what Goodlad and others call the "personal domain"--are not really passive recipients of the curriculum, but actively shape how the planned curriculum responds in the classroom to a live audience.

THE INSTITUTIONAL CURRICULUM

Like other technocrats in modern society, curriculum specialists can get lost in the technical aspects of curriculum and neglect the intellectual bases of what the school is trying to accomplish. The easiest example is for a curriculum development specialist to get lost in the long labyrinth of writing performance objectives and neglect the primary schooling goals. The curriculum, like a perpetual motion machine, can continue to operate on its own without anyone asking whether or not we even need one. This does not imply that we should treat lightly the pursuit of the goals of academic content. But we need to be mindful of the broader dimension of how germane the content of what schools teach is, and how different are the students who inhabit school's corridors from students of just a few years ago. In short, the times have changed, but the curriculum largely has not.

The obvious disparity is the gap between diminishing learning skills among the schooling population and the unchanged status of the curriculum. One could argue that teachers, as the local managers of the curriculum, need to re-adjust the emphasis to accommodate these learning deficiencies among students. However, a similar argument could be advanced that school or school system curriculum specialists have overly stressed low level cognitive skills and neglected or minimized social and psychological needs in curriculum texts.

The greatest danger in managing the curriculum is that it becomes bureaucratized, institutionalized, unchangeable, and that the establishment of the techniques of administration becomes routine. This is always a greater danger in public service than in private enterprise because the outcomes are not directly linked to profits. The curriculum becomes, when bureaucratized, a form of social control over students. Ideally, managing the curriculum should be an exercise in providing, not a stylized and systematized regimen of content, but a set of flexible alternatives to both the content of learning and the process of growing up.

Good managers want efficiency in the operation of their systems. They want order, regularity, neatness if possible, and everything run on time. It is the mark of a good production supervisor. This technological proficiency borrowed from business found its way into the schools in the early part of the 20th century. The curriculum, like the schedule and plant management, is a component in the scheme to maintain efficiency, order, and control.

This mechanistic view would be denied by many educators. But the school as an institutionalized bureaucracy is an accepted fact of modern life. Thus, the school's goals to maintain its organizational status have assumed more importance than the functioning of the lives of its clients and employees. Technological efficiency keeps in check the attempts to make the system more responsive, and managing the curriculum has come to mean not changing it.

Realistic responses to some questions will help clarify the role of the school manager of the curriculum, and aid in administering responsibilities.

1. What do you need to know about specific subject content in order to manage curriculum well?

2. What would you need to know, or what would have to happen, for you to make a significant curriculum change?

3. What do you need to know about the curriculum support systems, such as personnel and the budget, to manage the curriculum? Does the budget determine the curriculum?

4. What ways do you decide that the present curriculum is satisfactory?

5. In spite of all the demands and constraints, what would you really like to do as a curriculum manager that you now believe you can't?

Institutional decisions about the curriculum are often the result of pressures in the community--programs for refugee children; a drug abuse education program; an intensive emphasis on civics or science.

Developing specific programs is difficult because society rarely outlines details of what it wants; the outcome comes through administrative dictate or legislative fiat. Governing bodies are rarely required to go beyond the rhetorical in delineating expectations. It is the school that must translate sensible activities from societal anxieties about some aspect of education, to make substance of the symbolism for change.

THE ROLE OF CURRICULUM SPECIALISTS

Curriculum specialists, as technicians in a bureaucracy, manage only narrow and restricted tasks related to limited cognitive structures, primarily language.

The contradiction in the role of the curriculum manager is that none can perform the needed service as society's representative of integrated learning. Managers, like teachers, can only fulfill the roles assigned them by the hierarchical organization. Neither is free to manage the process of learning as they might see suitable. They can only manage that part of the organized structure the school administration chooses. This sense of maintenance of the organizational structure of schooling, and the unitary conformity of the curriculum, keep alive the need for technical proficiency in managing the status quo. Technical expertise is not in itself unhealthy unless, as in formal schooling, it inhibits the cultivation of the complete person, and does not permit deviation from the traditional.

Curriculum supervisors are viewed as a part of the administrative, not the teaching staff, and for those teachers who attach great importance to that distinction, effectiveness is impaired by perceived distance from student contact. On the other hand, curriculum specialists feel like automobile mechanics: they are called upon to repair worn out parts when the whole engine needs re-designing.

Curriculum developers may not take advantage of their discretionary power to improve the curriculum climate. They may perceive, perhaps correctly, that their boundaries for initiative in reform and change are confined. They may, in fact, have limited roles, and because of their administrative dominance have a carefully defined marginal capacity in doing the curriculum.

Curriculum specialists, as an administrative position, was created because teachers didn't have the time to develop the curriculum. Now teachers when urged to use curricula developed by specialists do not feel obliged because they were often not consulted. Curriculum responsibility, as a consequence, has been removed from the classroom and many teachers, untrained in curriculum development, rely on the materials someone else produces. The administration actually encourages this practice, and hires supervisors to do the curriculum. For a combination of reasons, teachers feel that their choices in developing curricula for their own use have shrunk to adoption of curricula already developed.

CURRICULUM RESOURCE MANAGEMENT

Much of curriculum management is confined, paradoxically, to the closet, and is often associated with the administration of the resources. Curriculum resources are, indeed, abundant. The question is, are the right resources in the right hands at the right time. Improvements in information processing by computer will eventually help keep track of the ordering, distribution and storing of relevant curriculum guides and aids.

Economics also determines the amount and currency of such

materials. Everyone wants the latest handbooks, movies, tapes, and texts. But most schools have to be content with getting the most from limited funds, and then making the supplies stretch even further. Ideally, educational authorities will gradually develop promising textual material, complete with graphics, by computer, and simply revise as needed, thus eliminating the cost of excessive duplication.

While conducting a curriculum workshop for specialists a few years ago in the State of Maine, I surveyed the group of over 70 participants. One of the questions I asked was: "When money is available for curriculum development, for what is it usually spent?" Thirty-four percent said that money was spent on "materials (including texts)." It would seem that for many school systems managing the curriculum consists of purchasing texts.

In a related survey question, the respondents indicated that the greatest organizational constraint was lack of funds. However, with some candor, nearly a quarter of all respondents said the greatest obstacle was "lack of local leadership," a subject to which we now turn.

CURRICULUM LEADERSHIP

Curriculum leadership, and not merely the static management of the curriculum, is both a professional and community responsibility. In one school district in the Los Angeles area in which I was a consultant, the school decided to revise the curriculum. The district asked the teachers to present a collective plan on what they thought the schools should be teaching. Then, wisely, they also asked community representatives. Finally, the school brought the two schemes together, and of course they didn't compare at all. A combined team of teachers and parents in the community thrashed out the compromise formula. In the end, both parents and teachers were more committed to the result. This shared view of participation in the development of the curriculum was a novel experiment indicative of the need to involve parents in professional activities. The administration, as a result, received more support for other, more controversial proposals, after this fruitful participatory exercise.

The task of curriculum leadership can be the responsibility of one person, either administrator or teacher. This process goes on in endless small ways throughout a schooling year as teachers make improvements in learning activities, or adjustments in learning styles. Often, a major curriculum adjustment occurs because of one leader, and when that person leaves or receives a new position, the reformed curriculum simply disappears. One person sustains the impetus and the appearance of reform is illusory because others have not adopted the new package.

THE POLITICS OF REVISION

How does anyone solve the problem of synthesizing the curriculum into a coherent whole? The problem was central to the thinking of Johann Friedrich Herbart (1776-1841) whose principal curriculum thrust was the development of moral character. He wanted schooling to correlate all subjects. Herbart saw the isolation of subjects as the failure of education. We have witnessed the development of the sovereignty of subjects over the unity of objective. The principal role of leadership in curriculum development, it seems to me, is to provide the bases for alteration, to give the burden of evidence for proposing necessary modifications. If research suggests, with abundant evidence, that participation in learning has greater long term effectiveness and is more meaningful, why is there still an emphasis on direct instructional techniques?

The gap between research results about schooling and teachers has widened exponentially, in part because of the politics of conducting research by higher education and not school personnel, and by the inability to transmit research results into accepted practices.

Having become accustomed to published textbooks, schools have entered into an economic pact that is difficult to break. In practice, schools have abrogated their responsibility to develop useable curriculum and instead gone the easier, but more expensive route, of purchasing their most important commodity--the content of what they teach. The central question is this: If schools hypothetically had to abandon all textbooks, what would the curriculum be? The purchased book has in practice become the curriculum, and only a complete re-thinking of what we want the schools to teach will force us to come to grips with ultimate goals.

But books are only an expression of the knowledge-based curriculum. School faculties who have actively engaged in curriculum development as a group have concluded that the most important learning outcomes are skill-based. As a result, the content of a course was not the only shaper of purpose. The collegial shaping of new curriculum plan at the institutional or school level may do as much for consolidating teaching morale as it does for improving the curriculum.

One innovative school district I once worked with as a consultant went to the lengths of contracting with a renowned "think tank"--The Hudson Institute in the U.S.--to discover what the experts thought the world would be like thirty years in the future. They compared the results of predictions of the future with their present curriculum to see if their students were receiving the training necessary to cope with the world they would inhabit as adults. The school district revised based on these societal predictions of the future.

In sum, the curriculum is a machine in finely tuned balance, composed of working parts from society, the accepted foundations of knowledge, some learner needs, community values and interests. Managing this potpourri of ingredients may be assigned to one or more individuals within an institution. But it is a collective professional responsibility. The professional and technical aspects of managing the curriculum will not always relate with the social and political demands.

Chapter Ten

EVALUATING THE CURRICULUM

> "Cheshire Puss," Alice began, "would you tell me
> please, which way I ought to go from here?"
> "That depends a good deal on where you want to get
> to," said the Cat.
> "I don't much care where," said Alice.
> "Then it doesn't matter which way you go," said the Cat.
> "...so long as I get somewhere," Alice said as an
> explanation.
> "Oh, you're sure to do that," said the Cat, "if you only
> walk long enough."
>
> Lewis Carroll, ALICE'S ADVENTURES IN WONDERLAND

School evaluation of any kind is much more than precision in the choice and use of instruments that quantifies responses to questions. The most important decisions about a schooling program, like a curriculum, is not just whether or not it seems to work when it is completed, but if it doesn't work very well what should be done. Relatively speaking, the collection of information about a curriculum is the easy part. The difficult part is deciding what to do if it doesn't satisfy the clients or school audiences and the public.

It is important to distinguish several kinds of decisions typically encountered in evaluating a curriculum. The three kinds of decisions involve: I students; II courses or curriculum units or programs; and III administration.

I DECISIONS ABOUT STUDENTS

The first decision concerns the individual student. High levels of student achievement seem to indicate that the curriculum is meritorious. But if the student performs poorly or inadequately, we seek blame elsewhere than the curriculum: the home environment, the teaching, the student's lack of motivation, to name a few probable causes. We may shift the student to a less rigorous course, a remedial exploration of lower quality for the age group. We want precise information about individual performance, but also need to know a student's comparative ranking with students of similar age.

School related tests, as contrasted to intelligence tests, usually measure one or more of the following conditions: 1) achievement--the supposed level of knowledge a student has of a subject; 2) aptitude, or the ability of the student to learn; 3) basic skills, or the student's mastery of a technique, such as reading; and 4) interests.

When and if school test scores are released, the findings can be misleading. For sometimes students' scores are pooled, summed or averaged into a single score. Comparing averaged student scores between schools, or even comparing averaged scores of students within a school can imply that certain teachers or schools are more successful. The error lies in assuming that an aggregate score actually represents an ability level. Standardized test scores are based on the assumption that half the children will score above the average, and half below. Often, in publicizing test score results, raw scores are converted to percentile scores which is a numerical representation of where the student stands in relation to others who took that test. A score on a standardized test may not even correlate well with a student's grade. A standardized test score may not measure what has actually been taught, and is thus an imperfect measure of the curriculum.

The use of a school's testing program on individual and comparative student achievement levels should contain a variety of measures that will yield information on student strengths and weaknesses that the curriculum would then address. Thus, the curriculum is the response to data gathered on student needs, and is not necessarily a check on curriculum success or failure.

II DECISIONS ABOUT COURSES

The second type of decision about the curriculum relates to the course of study, and concerns decisions about content, materials, and techniques which are hopefully satisfactory for bringing about desired changes: increases in knowledge or improvement in skill or attitude.

The central purpose of course evaluation is to decide what chief effects the course has on pupil behavior, in knowledge, skill and attitude. Course evaluation is not simply to determine whether a curriculum is good or not, but which particular units need revision. The outcomes of student progress through a course are multifaceted, and should not be limited to a ready response. The facile but incorrect response, I believe, is to reduce all components of a course into a single grade, in effect masking the multiple outcomes of the course objectives into a single aggregate. It would be important to know how a course produces its intended effects, for example, and which aspects of the curriculum bring about that change.

Evaluating a course of studies can be assessing different kinds of curricular aspects.

1) The first kind of course evaluation, and the most meaningful, is an assessment of the differences in the course design from the intended objectives. Clearly, a course of studies that strays from its aims is suspect in its substance, and possibly ineffective. Either the instruction is awry or the objectives are wrong.

2) A second kind of course evaluation measures the degree of difference and effectiveness between parts of a course. Is the section on gravity in physics as coherent and effective as the section on electricity? Are there major time differences in instructing the different sections of a course? A section analysis raises questions about the relative value of a section to the whole course.

3) A third level of course evaluation pertains to the differences between items. Individual bits of transmitted knowledge can be weighed against each other to determine conformity to course objectives. I believe it is also

important to determine, by analyzing items within a course, which promote a learning skill, which an attitude, and which just memory.

All such assessments of a course of studies presumes that there will be different measures of student proficiency--such as standardized tests--as well as attitudinal measures. The general concept is for the curriculum evaluator to consider how a particular course develops the student's total learning progress.

Consequently, curriculum evaluation in essence must include data and feedback about a student's general understanding and attitudes, about progress towards the overall schooling goals, and not just the course objectives. Somehow the evaluation of the curriculum must always raise serious questions about where the school can improve the delivery of its curricular services. Difficult decisions that bring about curricular changes must often follow the testing results.

For example, what is the school's instrument for measuring how a student understands the application of principles in science? Is this ability one that comes about with the flash of a new insight, or does the curriculum prepare the understanding of principles one at a time for student consumption? Does the course build upon previous conceptual understanding from other courses in science? The development of higher order understandings among students is of substantive, not peripheral, interest to the curriculum evaluator. Such educational outcomes are more transferable to further study than factual material.

III ADMINISTRATIVE DECISIONS

The third type of decision is administrative and involves the whole school, area or region. Should the school order a particular set of published materials for reading or science? A school curriculum committee will need to make a collective judgment about program strengths and weaknesses for an entire unit that perhaps will remain in force for many years. Decisions about whether or not to install a new program in reading, or in math or science, typically involve a whole educational system.

The larger the battery of evaluation instruments used in gathering information about a curriculum project, the greater the degree of accuracy in deciding on project effectiveness. Achievement tests of students are the most commonly used. They are usually readily available and somewhat reliable pointers to success. They may be standardized, or norm-referenced, or locally developed for specific curriculum use. Questionaires, project developed cognitive tests, attitude and interest measures, biographic data, checklists, classroom climate inventories--all are helpful in analyzing a curriculum project.

I have included a sample evaluation checklist for curriculum units. It is a relatively painless way of assessing how acceptable a text or unit might be, and a way of obtaining some consensus on desirable use.

However, the major administrative decisions, it seems to me, are the managing of what the principal curriculum goals are. This includes seeking the collective advice of the teaching faculty and the appropriate community members. Designing instruments for measuring effectiveness may appear difficult and tedious, and indeed it is. But attempting to evaluate a curriculum program that has ambiguous goals and strategies is more hopeless.

The idea of the curriculum as an experiment in learning is a contemporary idea, both novel and intriguing. It is an idea blended from science and psychology, and has at least theoretically replaced the concept

SAMPLE SET OF VARIABLES -- FOR CURRICULUM DEVELOPMENT

LEARNING MODE

Personality Style

Sociocultural Relevance

Cognitive Style
  Verbal Behavior
  Encoding Pattern
  Decoding Pattern
  Readiness
  Application
  Aptitude
  Interest

Rate of learning

Quality of Time on Task

Environmental Conditions

Psychological and Social Conditions

CURRICULUM

Cognitive Skills
  Reading
  Writing
  Speaking
  Listening

Psychomotor Skills

Social Skills

Academic Areas

Participation and Interest Areas

TEACHING MODE

Teaching Style
Diagnosis of Learning Ability
Technical Skills
  Humor
  Questioning Strategies
  Application Skills
  Frames of Reference
  Use of Examples
  Use of Themes
  Closure
  Maintenance of Interest
Grouping Practices
  Large Group
  Small Group
  Laboratory
  Independent Study
Management of Instruction
  Control of Participation
  Rewards and Sanctions
Evaluation
  Of Student Progress
  Of Curriculum
  Of Teaching

of the curriculum as dogma, in which any deviation is viewed as heretical. Perceptions of the content of the curriculum have changed because of the more widely accepted value of scientific inquiry, and the psychological value of differing modes of learning. The curriculum will always retain some static elements. But because of emerging objectives, organizational patterns, and evaluation procedures, experiment is now a part of the whole process of evaluating the curriculum. Evaluation, and all its attendant methodological tools, is an experimental process in deciding how best to instruct, transmit knowledge, and develop skills and attitudes among students, and under what conditions.

An evaluation of any kind and at any level has to be interpretable and believable. Something must have happened and the effects observed. And there must be some evidence that effects occurred because of some intervention (the curriculum, the teacher), and that these effects probably would not have occurred without the intervention.

Are things better than what you might have expected if the intervention had not occurred? Some growth or change will occur in spite of the evaluator's intervention, but how much? The trick is to find the most believable comparison that will confirm that the curriculum has been an improvement. A sound evaluation will control for the effects of other interventions, or possible reasons that do not include the curriculum, for the observed effects.

The evaluator's main question is: Did a change occur? The possible changes are in learner abilities or needs, teacher competencies, parent expectations, a lessening of student disruptions, etc. The second concern is for the evaluator to determine the evidence for the change. Are there valid and reliable measures for the changes? (A measure is valid if it has a logical relationship with what is measured. It is reliable, in the researcher's lexicon, if it measures, or ranks, consistently over and over the same things.) What are the best estimates of what would have occurred without the intervention, like the curriculum?

Other relevant questions for the curriculum evaluator include: Was the effect observed often enough, and was the effect consistent enough to be significant? Was the principal effect academically significant? Can the curriculum be conducted elsewhere with similar results? How likely is it that the results are directly attributable to the intervention of this curriculum? Is there enough evidence to make a reasonable judgment, or is the conclusion based on guesses and hopes? Are the final judgments consistent with the available evidence?

Evaluating a curriculum also means determining the degree of student interest. When the world of the student adolescent collides with the traditional formed world of the school curriculum the result is often aversion. How do you make a student enjoy math when interest is absent? The value of a curriculum evaluation, intellectually appealing as it may be to developers and teachers, begins negatively with disinterested students unless subject motivation exercises are included. Thus, evaluating the success of any curriculum must include the disposition of the students prior to involvement.

This general lack of student interest in specific subjects, or in schooling, may also be reflective of the clash of social values of the student, and the student's home environment, with that of the school. For the poor, for minorities, for the linguistically different, the school curriculum may be perceived as containing little cultural value. An inherently good and consistent curriculum must also be tailored to an extremely diverse schooling audience. But as noted elsewhere in this book, what is needed is multiple, not standard, uniform, approaches to content. The integrity of the curriculum can be maintained while experimentation continues with a range of ways of achieving skill objectives. A curriculum evaluation can assess this if one of the objectives of the curriculum is experimentation in delivery.

The relationships between social class, language, and socialization patterns can clearly influence the curricular impact on the student's consciousness. The teacher role is crucial. For example, the child's performance in the language of the school can determine how the teacher evaluates understanding of the curriculum, and this in turn leads to teacher expectations about future student performance. A curriculum evaluation that only factored in student achievement might lose the residual effect of other social determinants.

Based partly on language and on the knowledge of the parents' social class, teachers soon begin to classify students into categories like "bright" and "dull," and expectations about performance may thus prejudge actual ability, or prohibit the cultivation of native talent. So that no matter how wonderful one may think the packaged curriculum is, the behavior of the teacher weighs heavily in the scale of measuring curriculum effectiveness.

Moreover, the language of the teacher is a related factor in evaluating the curriculum. Teachers may believe that they are giving good instructions, when in fact students may be bewildered by what is expected of them, and confused about directions. Students often have perfectly logical answers for responses which may be incorrect for the teacher, and the fault lies in the teacher's lack of clarity.

Evaluation of schooling and curriculum and the assessment of student progress has expanded in recent decades because of the increase in the technical proficiency of statistics and quantification methods. But for all the scientific data available, a kind of art is still needed to interpret the data, for there are widely differing interpretations for collected statistical evidence and even for the power of the statistical measurement capacity. National surveys of students were conducted in the U.S. for *Project Talent* in the late 1950s; for what became know as the Coleman Report for the Civil Rights Act in the mid 1960s; and for the former Title I (now Chapter I) of the Elementary and Secondary Education Act, and the statistical results were criticized as much on technical grounds as were their conclusions. The most precise methodology is still open to interpretation.

Still, the evaluation process is now an accepted part of curriculum development. If a curriculum unit is assessed in view of the program's goals, and not overly obscured with quantified data, the evaluation can reveal substantive strengths and weaknesses.

Besides improvements in mathematical precision, curriculum evaluation has expanded because of the demand by the proprietors of programs--mainly governmental agencies--for believable evidence of a program's market authenticity. Do programs for disadvantaged children, or the linguistically different, really work? Does the math program actually increase math ability? The money expended in large scale curriculum programs presumes field testing and reasonable evidence of acceptance of the intended audience.

Curriculum content is developed, perhaps re-organized, packaged, tested, and eventually distributed. It is big business to publishers whose relationship to schools is economically symbiotic. Schools benefit because full-time specialists are costly.

Evaluating the curriculum is a game filled with pitfalls and potential hazards. The most common error is to assume that a gain in student scores is attributable only to the curriculum unit, or that improvement in grade equivalent scores in one grade means that the curriculum is better. Comparing inappropriate grade levels is another common error.

There are many tests which measure a student's cognitive development, and few that assess progress in psychological--like emotional satisfaction and attitude--or psychomotor skill improvement while undergoing a curriculum unit. I also believe that it is important to make some determination about all aspects of student development to some degree--affective, career and ethical--for every course. Emphasizing only cognition skills to the exclusion of the totality of human progress through a course is a narrow definition of evaluation.

On the other hand, the use of sensible evaluation techniques for improving an existing program through modification while a course is in progress--what is known as formative evaluation (summative evaluation occurs only at the end of a course or program)--can bring positive results. Here are some suggestions. Seek data only on the students in the course. Look for multi-dimensional outcomes, and map these separately. Identify which aspects can be revised and which cannot. Start collecting evidence during the course, and look for alternatives to possible effectiveness, like the skill of the teacher. Make use of some informal teacher reports. And make a process study of the classroom effects to measure proficiency and attitude changes. Lastly, look for special outcomes; for example: did the teacher become disinterested during the unit? Was the experience interrupted by a long holiday vacation? Did the appearance of a guest speaker change motivation towards the curriculum unit?

Evaluation constitutes only one part, although an integral one, of a school's program. The assessment process is primarily concerned with programs, of which student achievement gain may only be a part. It may be more meaningful for a student to gain an interest in a subject than initially to score high on achievement in it. But such attitudinal changes will not be readily known unless evaluation techniques to acquire relevant student information, not just achievement statistics, are conducted on a periodic basis.

The curriculum is essentially history...what the present generation knows of the past, and chooses to transmit to its youth. Evaluating the curriculum is a test to determine how successful both the teaching and the content have been. But evaluation, as an exercise in itself, is of little consequence unless goals have been previously identified.

Epilogue

> There is not to be too much *teaching*. What the
> children crave and need is experience. The school's
> main task is to supply opportunities.
> Bobbitt, *The Curriculum* (1918)

"Sixteen percent of white adults, forty-four percent of blacks, and fifty-six percent of Hispanic citizens are functional or marginal illiterates," says Jonathan Kozol in *Illiterate America*. The number of people, Kozol says, who cannot read at an adult level represents about a third of the entire adult population.

If the truth of this assertion, based on respectable evidence, is even close to the reality, then how could anyone claim that the curriculum of schools is adequate to preparing people for the demands of this technological society? The truth is the curriculum process in most schools is an institutionalized, mechanical, inflexible fixity, unresponsive to client and societal demands.

A few years ago, while acting as a consultant for the Kettering Foundation in a large inner-city high school in Washington D.C. which at the time was experimenting with student participation in curriculum development, I questioned the teachers about what they thought was the biggest problem in their school. There was general unanimity: the students couldn't read. I asked one teacher what she was doing about the reading problem. "I teach music," was the reply. I asked another: "I teach history." A third said that he taught English and was not a reading specialist. The point was clear: no one accepted the responsibility for teaching students to read because they had to teach their subjects.

Thus, the dilemma in curriculum is a fixation on subjects as the only curriculum thrust or delivery, and an inadvertent ignoring of the real learning needs of students. If identified students do not have the requisite learning skills (as distinct from the factual recall of knowledge) then any further agenda in the planned lessons ceases. What ensues is that the curriculum focuses exclusively on the acquisition of learning skills, but especially literacy, numeracy, and fundamental civic and political understandings. Skills development--and clearly reading assumes major importance--becomes the curriculum action. A fourteen year old adolescent, who is semi-literate, needs intensive coaching and attention in reading, and not in the subject of the class hour. The tired, old cliche from teachers that they have other students to teach and supervise, and cannot attend to the needs of just one student who is "behind," just doesn't wash.

School evaluations need to report on student progress in learning skill development, not simply grades in a discipline of knowledge. The curriculum needs also to emphasize the affective domain--not usually found in textbooks--as a significant ingredient in the maturation of youth, and not just cognitive skill development.

Throughout this book I have not meant to underplay the importance of a solid knowledge basis for students. What I have done is emphasize the basis for acquiring knowledge--the tools or skills of learning, because I believe that schools tend to neglect these primary conditions for a person extending the power and capability to improve the ways and dimensions for knowing.

The curriculum, as understood by schools, needs to be free of its institutional constraints, and to be channeled to satisfy individual learning needs. Schools need to experiment with scheduling innovations, instructional grouping practices, differentiation in teaching responsibilities other than "classrooms," and variability in salary schedules. The orthodoxy of the standard schooling organization pattern is inhibitive of change. Like hospitals, schools need more emergency rooms, trauma centers, and behavior modification programs.

The loss of literacy is only the first erosion in a curriculum process which fails to respond to the necessity of building on where the student is in time, in place, and in maturational development. The assignment of curriculum matter must first begin with an assessment of learning conditions.

The curriculum, as understood by schools, needs to be free of its institutional constraints, and to be channeled to satisfy individual learning needs. The loss of literacy is only the first erosion in a curriculum process which fails to respond to the necessity of building on where the student is in time, in place, and in maturational development. The assignment of curriculum matter must first begin with an assessment of learning conditions.

The curriculum as it exists in schools is flawed because it doesn't apply to students, or at least teachers don't lead students to the application phase of learning. Too much is simple memory recall, and little time is spent on comprehension, or application, or synthesis, or evaluative judgment. Students can be creative by writing personal experiences before learning the rules of grammar. They can observe, and begin to ask questions, before they learn the theories of science. They can experiment with electrical equipment before they understand what electricity is. Building in the higher order processes at the beginning of curriculum units allows the instructor to lay the framework for these processes to take root eventually. Never teaching for them is a potentially damaging learning disability for the students, and a gross professional omission.

The curriculum, both collectively and individually within any subject area, should always point to something, should lead to the unknown, to a positive attitude towards learning even in spite of student low achievement in a subject. Like the exact meaning of "commencement," which as educators we use so blithely at the end of the schooling year, so the curriculum should never lead to a conclusion, but to a beginning; not to the end of a test, but to more questions, to the application of knowledge in the occupational world, to how what we learn can help us as adults.

Schools tend to duck and take cover when it comes to discussing the real societal issues, like social class and social interactions. Students have un-refined and ambiguous emotional responses to differences in society, yet they readily label students within their closed schooling culture. Contemporary definitions include: jocks, nerds, acid heads, freaks, and preppies. Since basic communications skills, much less social interaction skills, like group behavior, are not courses as such, they are only rarely a curriculum matter. They may be schooling goals, but that is quite another concern, since schooling goals rarely get translated into curriculum objectives.

Character development, moreover, also does not assume major dominance because it too is not a course objective, nor are curriculum units planned for it. The characters in novels or short stories are studied, but not the characters in the classroom. Thus, character development, however it may be envisaged, is another neglected but relevant curriculum topic. Although much lauded in the abstract--except in religious schools-- character development is too often associated with moral or religious development and hence avoided as too controversial. As a result, students never learn that a person can be righteous and ethical without even being religious, or that they can have a respectable character disassociated from a religious affiliation. Or conversely, that they can be very religious, but not moral.

Ultimately, schools sidestep the issue of helping shape a young person's personality, by emphasizing chiefly cognitive development. Rhetoric about schooling objectives to the contrary, classes and the curriculum are about academic subjects, and the teaching of subject disciplines. The teaching of values, and the planning for instruction in values, are too essential to be dodged by unimaginative curriculum thinking. The development of a young person's values is crucial to adult life, and for the school to hide behind a cloak of neutrality regarding this aspect of development is professionally irresponsible.

What I am speaking to is direct instruction about values, preferably by means of a questioning strategy. Schools, of course, do teach values... in the way they do business. In general, schools inculcate a definite value system, for the most part the dominant religious sentiments of the region where the school is located. The values are religious in origin, although not necesarily theologically distinct by known or identifiable religious affiliation. They are in general Protestant. The controversy over prayer, textbooks, evolution, sex, and scores of other societal dilemmas attest to the hesitancy of school administrators to deal overtly with anything like "values." The standards of the community become the curriculum standards for the school, and for anyone to pretend that those schooling values are purely secular does not know history or schools.

Sadly and ironically, the operating curriculum is like an adolescent: naive and innocent of the world, of relationships, of a mature response to the processes for improvement. The quality of a curriculum is in its (to borrow a term from national defense strategy) flexible response to diverse needs, and not in its uniform delivery of standardized knowledge. What counts for a quality curriculum, to use a medical analogy again, is not the pill itself, but the diagnosis and the prescription together.

If effective learning is to occur, then both students and teacher must agree on the objectives to be reached, and on the conditions necessary to sustain motivation and interest. I have defined the curriculum as what the teacher does. The conditions of learning include both the management of instruction and student behavior. My own teaching preference would be to keep a few key ideas in mind while cultivating a climate of persistent questions and questioning, and to eschew sequential outlines and long lists of data...an easy trap to fall into in geology and history. The trick is to avoid superficiality from students by not tolerating mediocrity in teaching performance. Students deserve answers to why a subject is necessary, even if they've heard it before. Unfortunately, the reasons given are too shallow and hurried, as if unimportant, when in fact they form the basis for studying a lesson in the first place. The incentives for learning come first.

The subject will never connect with the students--and there are more of them than we want to admit who are withdrawn, wary, impassive, full of ennui--unless the teacher as mediator plays a forceful and commanding role in building trust and acceptance as a friend. Large blocks of students have learned the game of school by dodging the difficult part of disciplined inquiry, of minimum risk, of just getting by. For them the teacher challenge is engagement: in activity, in probing themselves, in putting forward. It is the beginnings of tentative thought, which all adolescents want to hide, that needs exposure. The skillful teacher will not allow learning masks to form (or worse to harden) around the dodging mind. I would have each student prepare a curriculum unit and teach it in every class.

But the example of the non-participating student is a common one, and symptomatic of a condition in the developing personality which extends beyond the classroom, perhaps even beyond the school. Nevertheless, these personality conditions and causes, especially in the maturing adolescent, need a trusting teacher, a caring adult. The role of the teacher as therapist, as coach, as adult role model, is under-rated in the profession.

The passion that adolescents can exhibit in nearly any activity-- sports, extracurricular activities, popular music, social affairs--is not channeled in classroom activities. There are tests, assignments, required attention, exercises. The most careless teachers, and the most insecure in personality, will use threats as a way of bolstering their authority, and will often humiliate students in a playful way. The resentment this builds undermines the fruitful motivation required. It also sends the wrong signal that power is the game and not cooperative learning in a positive environment where mutual trust reigns.

Clearly, curriculum cannot be disassociated from all schooling elements--the administration of the school; the quality of teachers and teaching; the community it serves; the salary schedule; and, most importantly, the nature of the attending students. Curriculum is a locked-in component, often subject to events beyond its strict purview or limited dominion. Yet its scope, its structure, its delivery, is at the core of what schools are about. The curriculum should be the single most powerful force in the school's total program, to which all other influences are, ironically, secondary.

At the classroom level the most ignored learning principle, upon which the selection and organization of curricular content is based, is the proper diagnosis of needs and learning status. Despite protestations from educational psychologists, researchers and educational leaders to the contrary, the majority of "lesson plans" still consist of building on the academic subject matter to the exclusion of probable learning needs at the skill and proficiency levels of mastery. In this sense, curriculum is still viewed as plans, and not primarily as diagnosis of level of ability.

Students now in school will be addressing over the next half century issues vital to the quality of life on planet earth and of its people. The issues have already been identified, but they will become more pronounced in the near future. The concerns are: the reduction of the earth's ozone layer; the explosion of human population in the developing world (the population reached 5 billion in mid-1986); the serious depletion of the earth's forests and tree cover; the spread of infectious diseases, like AIDS, for which there is no known cure; the global warming trend, because of excessive application of chlorofluorocarbons, and its impact on natural and biological systems; nuclear radiation as peacetime power use; resource demands on over-burdened urban centers, most of which are in the Third World. Present efforts to improve the quality of life are failing as the biosystem of the total earth is threatened with expanding and careless human activity.

Can a general education fail to take into account these fundamental adjustments in the earth, in its people, and in the future?

Curriculum revolution must come both internally and externally: from the temperature of the times, to inspired leadership at the school level.

Externally, the world has changed in profound ways in the last few decades. Stresses on the ecosystem are reaching points of destabilization throughout the developing world. Real economic gains will deteriorate in the near future with rising oil costs, and the depletion of petroleum reserves, a constant climatic warming trend (because of increased carbon deposits in the atmosphere), and diminishing forest and soil cover. The world will soon desperately need environmental reform in food production, population control, energy, and economics. And all this barring any increase in military confrontations.

Increased population and competition for resources is not just a science topic in the curriculum. It is a part of literate knowledge. The nature of these dramatic planetary changes will change the world order, and those currently in school will have to confront them as adults.

In the industrialized world, there is evidence of some slippage in overall schooling achievement. In the developing world, compulsory education has become a cruel charade as the schooling population has outstripped the scarce educational resources. The irony is that because of the inadequacy of schooling in the most populated developing countries, and the disproportionate increase in school-aged population, there is now more ignorance in the world than ever before in human history.

The curriculum is not just a stale academic pursuit. It is the central core of the schooling program, part of an international drama to uplift the knowledge industry and to maintain high levels of general literacy, upon which the information age is grounded, and to broaden the ability of the next generation to respond vigorously to the planet's present and future dilemmas.

Like the global environment, schools and the curriculum are eroding in robustness. Both need substantive and radical changes in policy, and flexibility in design.

Bibliography

Adler, M. (1982) *The Paedeia Proposal*, New York, Macmillan, 1982
Anastasi, A. (1958) *Differential Psychology* (3rd edition), New York, Macmillan
Ausubel, D. (1965) *Educational Psychology: A Cognitive View* , New York, Holt Rinehart and Winston
Babbie, E. R. (1979) *The Practice of Social Research*, Belmont, Wadsworth
Barnes, B. R. and E. U. Clawson (1975) 'Do Advance Organizers Facilitate Learning: Recommendations for Further Research Based on an Analysis of 32 Studies, *Review of Educational Research*, vol. 45, no. 4
Beauchamp, G. A. (1961) *Curriculum Theory*, Wilmette, Illinois, The Kagg Press
Beauchamp, G. A. (1975) *Curriculum Theory*, Evanston, Illinois, The Kagg Press
Belth, M. (1965) *Education as a Discipline*, Boston, Allyn & Bacon
Blenkin, G. M., and A.V. Kelly (1981) *The Primary Curriculum*, London, Harper and Row
Bloom, B. S. *et al.* (1956) *Taxonomy of Educational Objectives, Handbook I: Cognitive Domain*, New York, David McKay
Bloom, B. S. (1976) *Human Characteristics and School Learning*, New York, McGraw Hill
Bobbitt, F. (1918) *The Curriculum*, Boston, Houghton Mifflin
Bonnycastle, J. (1819) *An Introduction To Mensuration and Practical Geometry* (12th edition), London, Longman & Co.
Borg, W. and M.Gall (1979) *Educational Research* (3rd edition), New York, Longmans.
Boston, B. (1977) *Education Policy and the Education for All Handicapped Children Act*, Washington, D. C., Institute for Educational Leadership, The George Washington University
Bronowski, J. (1956) *Science and Human Values*, New York, Julian Messner
Brown, S. (1976) 'Discovery and Teaching A Body of Knowledge', *Curriculum Theory Network*, vol. 5, no. 3
Bruner, J. S. (1960,1962) *The Process of Education*, Cambridge, Harvard University Press
Bruner, J. S. (1966) *Toward A Theory of Instruction*, Cambridge, Harvard University Press
Burns, R. N. and G. D. Brooks (1970) *Curriculum Design in a Changing Society*, Englewood Cliffs, N.J., Education Technology Publications
Butterfield, H. (1957) *The Origins of Modern Science 1300-1800*, New York, The Free Press
Campbell, D.T. and J.C. Stanley (1963) 'Experimental and Quasi-Experimental Designs for Research on Teaching' in N.L. Gage (ed.), *Handbook for Research on Teaching*, Chicago, Rand McNally
Case, R. (1975) 'Gearing the Demands of Instruction to the Developmental Capacities of the Learner', *Review of Educational Research*, vol. 45, no. 1
Charters, W.W. (1923,1971) *Curriculum Construction*, New York, Arno Press and the New York Times
Charters, W.W. and N.L. Gage (eds.) (1963) *Readings in the Social Psychology of Education*, Boston, Allyn and Bacon.
Coleman, J. (1975) 'Methods and Results in the IEA Studies of Effects of School on Learning', *Review of Educational Research*, vol.12, no.3
Coleman, J.S. *et al.* (1966) *Equality of Educational Opportunity*, Washington D.C., U.S. Government Printing Office
College Entrance Examination Board (1966) *The Challenge of Curricular*

Change, New York

Conant, J. B. (1961) *Slums and Suburbs*, New York, McGraw Hill Book Co.

Conant, J.B. (1963) *The Education of American Teachers*, New York, McGraw Hill

Connor, F. P. and M. Cohen (1973) *Leadership Preparation for Educators of Crippled and Other Health Impaired-Multiply Handicapped Populations*, Washington, D.C., Bureau of Education for the Handicapped, U.S. Office of Education

Cooley, W. (1976) 'Implications of the Harnischfeger-Wiley Model for Research on Learning and Instruction', *Curriculum Inquiry*, vol. 6, no. 1

Cooper, J.M. (ed.) (1972) *Differentiated Staffing*, Philadelphia, W.B. Saunders

Cronbach, L. J. (1963) 'Evaluation for Course Improvement,' *Teachers College Record*, vol. 64, no.8

Cremin, L.A. (1961) *The Transformation of the School: Progressionism in American Education 1876-1957*, New York, Knopf

Darwin, Charles (1952) *The Origin of the Species by means of Natural Selection*, Chicago, Encyclopedia Britannica

Darwin, Charles (1896) *The Descent of Man and Selection in Relation to Sex*, New York, D. Appleton & Co.

Deloria, V. Jr. (1969) *Custer Died for your Sins*, London, Colier Macmillan

Deloria, V. Jr. (1973) *God is Red*, New York, Grosset & Dinlap

Deno, E. (1971) *Instructional Alternatives for Exceptional Children*, Reston, The Council for Exceptional Children

Descartes, Rene (1952) *Discourse on the Method of Rightly Conducting the Reason and Seeking the Truth in the Sciences*, Chicago, Great Books of the Western World

Dewey, John (1916) *Democracy and Education*, New York, The Macmillan Co.

Dewey, John (1938) *Experience and Education*, New York, The Macmillan Co.

Dewey, John (1960) *The Child and the Curriculum and School and Society*, Chicago, University of Chicago Press

Durant, Will and Ariel (1968) *The Lessons of History*, New York, Simon and Shuster

Dusek, J. B. (1975) 'Do Teachers Bias Children's Learning?', *Review of Educational Research*, vol. 45, no. 4

Eble, K. (1966) *A Perfect Education*, New York, Macmillan Co

Edelfelt, R. and E. B. Smith (1978) *Breakaway to Multi-dimensional Approaches, Integrating Curriculum Development and Inservice Education*, Washington D.C., Association of Teacher Educators

Edman, I. (1956) *The Works of Plato*, New York, Modern Library

Educating Children with Special Needs, Current Trends in School Policies and Programs (1974), Arlington,Va., National School Public Relations Association

Einstein, A. (1945) *The Meaning of Relativity*, Princeton, N.J., University Press

Eiseley, L.(1969) *The Unexpected Universe*, New York, Harcourt Brace & World

Eisner, E. and E. Vallance (1974) *Conflicting Conceptions of Curriculum*, Berkeley, McCutchan Publishing Co.

Eisner, E. (1979) *The Educational Imagination*, New York, Macmillan

Eisner, E. (1979) *Confronting Curriculum Reform*, Boston, Little, Brown & Co.

Ellis, J. A. and W. H. Wulfech and W. E. Montague (1980) 'The Effect of Adjunct and Test Question Similarity on Study Behavior and Learning in a Training Course', *American Educational Research Journal*, vol.17, no. 4

English, F. W. (1978) *Quality Control in Curriculum Development*, Arlington,Va., American Association of School Administrators

Erickson, D.A. (1976) 'Implications for Organizational Research of the Harnischfeger-Wiley Model', *Curriculum Inquiry*, vol. 6, no. 1

Fenstermacher, G. D. and J. I. Goodlad (eds.) (1983) *Individual Differences and the Common Curriculum*, Chicago, University of Chicago Press

Firth, G.R. and R.B Kingston (1973) *The Curriculum Continuum in Perspective*, Itasca,Illinois, F.E. Peacock Publishers

Flanders, N. A. (1979) *Analyzing Teacher Behavior*, Reading, Mass., Addison-Wesley

Forcese, D. P. and S. Richer (1973) *Social Science Methods*, Englewood Cliffs, N.J.,Prentice Hall

Foskett, D. J. (1965) *How to Find Out: Educational Research*, Oxford, Pergamon Press

Freire, Paulo (1974) *The Pedagogy of the Oppressed*, New York, The Seabury Press

Functions of the Placement Committee in Special Education, A Resource Manual (1976), Washington D.C., National Association for State Directors of Special Education

Galbraith, J. K. (1977) *The Age of Uncertainty*, Boston, Houghton Mifflin & Co.

Gallagher, D. and I. (1962) *The Education of Man, The Educational Philosophy of Jaques Mountain*, Garden City, Doubleday & Co.

Giroux, HA. and A. N. Penna and W. F. Pinar (1981) *Curriculum and Instruction, Alternatives in Education*, Berkeley, California, McCutchan Publishing Co.

Glass, B.(1959) *Science and Liberal Education*, Baton Rouge, Louisiana State University Press

Good, C. V. (1966) *Essentials of Educational Research*, New York Appleton-Century-Croft

Goodlad, J. and Associates (1979) *Curriculum Inquiry*, New York, McGraw Hill

Goodlad, J. (1984) *A Place Called School*, New York, McGraw Hill

Gordon, P.(ed.) (1981) *The Study of the Curriculum*, London, Batsford

Gress, J. R. and D. E. Purpel (1978) *Curriculum, An Introduction to the Field*, Berkeley, California, McCutchan Publishing Co.

Gutek, G. L. (1972) *A History of the Western Educational System*, New York, Random House

Hallinan, M. (1976) 'Salient Features of the Harnishfeger-Wiley Model', *Curriculum Inquiry*, vol. 6, no. 1

Hanley, J. P. and E. W. Moo (1970) *Curiosity, Competence, Community, Man: A Course of Study, An Evaluation*, Cambridge, Educational Development Center

Harnischfeger, A. and D. E. Wiley (1976) 'The Teaching-Learning Process in Elementary Schools: A Synoptic View', *Curriculum Inquiry*, vol. 6 no. 1

Havighurst, R. J. (1981) 'Indian Education: Accomplishments of the Last Decade', *Phi Delta Kappan*,vol. 62, pp. 329-31

Hayman, J. L. (1968) *Research in Education*, Columbus, Charles Merrill Publishing Co.

Heath, R. W. (1964) *New Curricula*, New York, Harper and Row

Henry, J.(1971) *Jules Henry on Education*, New York, Random House

Highet, G. (1955) *The Art of Teaching*, New York, Vintage Books

Hilgard, E.R. and R.C. Atkinson and R.L Atkinson (1971) *Introduction to Psychology* (5th edition), New York

Hilgard, E. R. (1964) 'The Place of Gestalt Psychology and Field Theories in Contemporary Learning Theory' in E.R. Hilgard (ed.), *Theories of Learning and Instruction*, Chicago, University of Chicago Press

Hilgard, E. R. and G. H. Bower (1966) *Theories of Learning* (3rd edition), New York, St. Martins Press

Hillway, T. (1969) *Handbook of Educational Research*, Boston, Houghton Mifflin

Hirst, P. (1974) *Knowledge and the Curriculum*, London, Routledge & Kegan Paul

Holly, D. (1973) *Beyond Curriculum, Changing Secondary Education*, London, Hart-Davis, MacGibbon

Holt, J. (1964) *How Children Fail*, New York, Pittman

Holt, M. (1979) *Regenerating the Curriculum*, London, Routledge & Kegan Paul

Huebner, D.(1976) 'The Moribund Curriculum Field: Its Wake and our Work', *Curriculum Inquiry*, vol. 6, no. 2

Illich, I. (1970) *Deschooling Society*, New York, Harper and Row

Jeffreys, M.V.C. (1967) *John Locke, Prophet of Common Sense*, London, Methuen & Co.

Jencks, C. *et al.* (1972) *Inequality: A Reassessment of Family and Schooling in America*, New York, Basic Books

Jensen, A.R. (1967) 'How Much Can We Boost I.Q. and Scholastic Achievement?', *Harvard Educational Review*, vol. 39, no. 1

Jensen, A. R. (1979) *Bias in Mental Testing*, New York, The Free Press

Johnson, R.E. (1975) 'Meaning in Complex Learning', *Review of Educational Research*, vol. 45., no. 3

Joyce, B. (1971) 'The Curriculum Worker of the Future' in Robert McClure (ed.), *The Curriculum: Retrospect and Prospect*, 70th Yearbook, National Society for the Study of Education, Chicago, University of Chicago Press

Joyce, B. or M. Weil (1972) *Models of Teaching*, Englewood Cliffs, N.J., Prentice-Hall

Judson, H. F. (1980) *The Search for Solutions*, New York, Holt Rinehart and Winston

Kelly, A.V. (1980) *Curriculum Context*, London, Harper & Row

Kifes, E. (1973) 'Relationship Between Academic Achievement and Personality Characteristics: A Quasi-Longitudinal Study', *AERJ*, vol. 12, no.2

King, A. B. and J. A. Brownell (1966) *The Curriculum and the Disciplines of Knowledge*, New York, John Wiley & Sons

Kirst, M. and Decker F. Walker (1971) 'An Anlaysis of Curriculum Policy-Making', *Review of Educational Research*, vol. 45, no. 5

Klosko, G.(1986) *The Development of Plato's Political Theory*, New York, Methuen

Kneller, G. (1965) *Educational Anthropology*, New York, John Wiley & Sons

Kohler, W.(1969) *The Task of Gestalt Psychology*, Princeton, N.J., Princeton University Press

Krathwohl, D. R. and B. Bloom and B. B. Masia (1964) *Taxonomy of Educational Objectives, II Affective Domain*, New York, David McKay

Kroeber, T. (1971) *Ishi in Two Worlds, A Biography of the Last Wild Indian in North America*, Berkeley, University of California Press

Lawton, Denis *et al.* (1978) *Theory and Practice of Curriculum Studies*, London, Routledge and Kegan Paul

Lewin, K. (1935) *A Dynamic Theory of Personality*, selected papers translated by Donald K. Adams, New York, McGraw Hill

Liston, D.P. (1986) 'On Facts and Values: An Analysis of Radical Curriculum Studies', *Educational Theory*, vol. 36, no. 2

Locke, John (1964) *Some Thoughts Concerning Education*, London, Heinemann

Locke, John (1714) *The Works of John Locke*, London, Churchill

Mager, R. F. (1962) *Preparing Instructional Objectives*, Palo Alto, California, Fearon Publishers

Mager, R. F. (1975) *Preparing Instructional Objectives* (2nd edition), Palo Alto, California, Fearon Publishers

Man: A Course of Study, Talks To Teachers (1968) Cambridge, Mass., Education Development Center

Man: A Course of Study, Seminar for Teachers (1970) Cambridge, Mass., Education Development Center

Man: A Course of Study, Talks To Teachers (1970) Cambridge, Mass., Education Development Center

Marrow, A. J. (1960) *The Practical Theorist, The Life and Work of Kurt Lewin*, New York, Basic Books

Martin, J. (1976) 'What Should We Do with a Hidden Curriculum When We Find One?' *Curriculum Inquiry*, vol. 6, no. 2

Mayer, R. E. (1975) 'Information Processing Variables in Learning to Solve Problems', *Review of Educational Research*, vol. 45, no. 4

McClure, R. M. (1971) *The Curriculum: Retrospect and Prospect*, 70th Yearbook, NSSE, Chicago, University of Chicago Press

McDermott, J. (1967) *The Writings of William James, A Comprehensive Edition*, New York, Random House

McDonald, J.B. (1971) 'Curriculum Theory', *Journal of Educational Research*, vol. 64, no. 5

McKeen, R. L. (1977) 'Behavioral Objectives and Non-Behavioral Objectives: A Case of When and Where', *College Student Journal*, vol.2, no. 2

McNeil, J. D. (1978) 'Curriculum-A Field Shaped By Different Faces', *Educational Researcher*, vol. 7, pp.19

McNeil, J. D. (1981) *Curriculum, A Comprehensive Introduction* (2nd edition), Boston, Little Brown & Co.

Meichenbaum, D.(1975) 'Enhancing Creativity By Modifying What Subjects Say to Themselves', *AERJ*, vol. 12, no.2

Messick, S. (1981) 'Evidence and Ethics in the Evaluation of Tests', *Educational Researcher*, vol. 10, pp. 9-20

Molner, A. and J. A. Zahorik (eds.) (1977) *Curriculum Theory*, Washington D.C., Association for Supervision and Curriculum Development

Morgan, J. E. (1936) *Horace Mann, His Ideas and Ideals*, Washington D.C., National Home Library Association

National Society for the Study of Education (1926) *The Foundations of Curriculum Making*, 26th Yearbook, Part II, Bloomington, Illinois, Public School Publishing Co.

National Society for the Study of Education (1953) *Adapting the Secondary School Program to the Needs of Youth*, 52nd Yearbook, Chicago, University of Chicago Press

National Society for the Study of Education (1971) *The Curriculum: Retrospect and Prospect*, 70th Yearbook, Chicago, University of Chicago Press

National Society for the Study of Education (1983) *Individual Differences and the Common Curriculum*, 82nd Yearbook, Chicago, University of Chicago Press

Nicholls, A. and S. Howard (1972) *Developing A Curriculum, A Practical Guide*, George Allen and Unwin

Phenix, P. (1961) *Education and The Common Good*, New York, Harper & Bros.

Phenix, P. (1964) *Realms of Meaning*, New York, McGraw Hill

Pinar, W. (1975) *Curriculum Theorizing*, Berkeley, California, McCutchan Publishing Co.

Pinar W. (1978) 'Notes on the Curriculum Field 1978', *Educational Researcher*, vol. 7, pp.5-12

Posner, G.J. (1974) 'The Extensiveness of Curriculum Structure: A Conceptual Scheme', *Review of Educational Research*, vol. 44, no.4

Postman, N. and C. Weingarten (1969) *Teaching As a Subversive Activity*, New York, Delacorte Press

Power, Edward J. (1969) *Evolution of Educational Doctrine: Major Educational Theorists of the Western World*, New York, Appleton-Century-Crofts

Price, K. (1962) *Education and Philosophical Thought*, Boston, Allyn & Bacon

Provus, M. (1972) *Discrepancy Evaluation*, Berkeley, California, McCutchan Publishing Co.

Randhawa, B. S. and J. O. Michayluk (1975) 'Learning Environment in Rural and Urban Classrooms', *AERJ*, vol. 12, no. 3

Raths, J. D. (1978) 'Encouraging Trends in Curriculum Evaluation', *Educational Leadership*, vol. 35, no. 4

Reynolds, M. and M. D. Davis (1972) *Exceptional Children in Regular Classrooms*, Washington D.C., Bureau of Adult and Occupational Education, U.S. Office of Education

Reynolds, M. (1975) *Special Education in School System Decentralization*, Washington D.C., Bureau of Adult and Occupational Education, U.S. Office of Education

Riesman, D. (with N. Blazer and R. Denney) (1964,1950) *The Lonely Crowd, A Study of the Changing American Character*, New Haven, Yale University Press

Rogers, Carl (1969) *Freedom To Learn*, Columbus, Ohio, Charles E. Merrill Publishing Co.

Rogers, C. (1951) *On Becoming A Person*, Boston, Houghton Mifflin Co.

Ross, A. O. (1976) *Psychological Aspects of Learning Disabilities and Reading Disorders*, New York, McGraw Hill

Rowntree, D. (1982) *Educational Technology in Curriculum Development*, London, Harper and Row

Rusk, R. R. (1969) *The Doctrine of the Great Educators* (4th edition), New York, St. Martin's Press

Ryan, K. (1975) *Teacher Education*, 74th Yearbook, NSSE, Chicago, University of Chicago Press

Saylor, G. J. and W. M. Alexander (1974) *Planning Curriculum for Schools*, New York, Holt Rinehart and Winston

Saylor, J. G. and W. M. Alexander and A. J. Lewis (1981) *Curriculum Planning for Better Teaching and Learning*, New York, Holt Rinehart and Winston

Sax, G. (1968) *Foundations of Educational Research*, Englewood Cliffs, N.J., Prentice Hall Inc.

Selakovich, D. (1984) *Schooling In America*, New York, Longmans

Sharpes, D. K. (1969) 'Differentiating Teachers and the Self-Fulfilling Hypotheses', *The California Journal for Instructional Development*, vol. 12, no. 4

Sharpes, D. K. with F. W. English (1972) *Strategies for Differentiated Staffing*, Berkeley, California, McCutchan

Sharpes, D.K. (1974) 'A New Curriculum Design for Native American Schools', *Indian Education Confronts the Seventies*, American Indian Resource Associates, Oglala, South Dakota, Vol. II

Sharpes, D. K. (1975) 'School Test Scores: What Do They Mean?', *The*

Virginia Globe, November 6

Sharpes, D. K. (1975) 'A Curriculum Model for American Indian Schools', *Educational Journal, Institute for the Development of Indian Law*, vol. 2, no. 9

Sharpes, D. K. (1976) 'A Developmental Curriculum for the Mildly Retarded of Intermediate and High School Age', *Education and Training of the Mentally Retarded*, vol. 11, no. 2

Sharpes, Donald K. (1978) 'A New Curriculum Design for American Indian Schools', *Journal of American Indian Education*, vol. 17, no. 2

Sharpes, D. K. (1979) 'Setting Up A Program for Disruptive Students in a Rural School System', *American School Board Journal*,vol. 166, no. 10

Sharpes, D. K. (1979) 'Federal Education for the American Indian', *Journal of American Indian Education*, vol. 19, no. 1

Shipman, M. D. (1974) *Inside a Curriculum Project*, London, Methuen and Co. Ltd.

Silberman, C.E. (1970) *Crisis in the Classroom*, New York, Random House

Sizer, T. (1984) *Horace's Compromise, The Dilemma of The American High School*, Boston, Houghton Mifflin

Skinner, B.F. (1968) *The Technology of Teaching*, New York, Appleton-Century-Crofts

Smith, H.A. (1969) 'Curriculum Development and Instructional Materials', *Review of Educational Research*, vol. 39, no.4

Sockett, H.(1976) *Designing The Curriculum*, London, Open Books

Spencer, H. (1906) *Education; Intellectual Moral and Physical*, London, Watts & Co.

Spencer, H. (1861) *Education; Intellectual, Moral and Physical*, London, Watts & Co.

Stake, K. (1975) 'The Logic of Learning By Discovery', *Review of Educational Research*, vol. 45, no. 3

Stallings, J. (1980) 'Allocated Academic Learning Time Revisited, or Beyond Time on Task', *Educational Researcher*, vol. 9, pp. 11-16

Szasz, M. C. (1974,1977) *Education and the American Indian*, Albuquerque, New Mexico, University of New Mexico Press

Taba, H. (1962) *Curriculum Development: Theory and Practice*, New York, Harcourt, Brace and Jovanovich

Tanner, D. and L. N. Tanner (1980) *Curriculum Development* (2nd edition), New York, Macmillan

Teeter, R. (1983) *The Opening Up of American Education, A Sampler*, New York, University Press of America

Thelen, H. (1960) *Education and the Human Quest*, New York, Harper and Row

Travers, R. M. W. (1969) *An Introduction to Educational Research* (3rd edition), New York, Macmillan

Tyler, R. (1950) *Basic Principles of Curriculum and Instruction*, Chicago, University of Chicago Press

Unruh, G. (1975) *Responsive Curriculum Development*, Berkeley, California, McCutchan

U.S. Senate (1969) *Indian Education: A National Tragedy, A National Challenge*, 91st Congress

Valpy, R. (with additions by C. Anthon) (1830) *The Elements of Greek Grammar*, New York, Collins & Co.

Vantil, W. (1976) *Issues in Secondary Education*, 75th Yearbook, NSSE, Chicago, University of Chicago Press

Vernant, J. (1982) *The Origins of Greek Thought*, Ithaca, N.Y. Cornell University Press

Walker, D.F. (1974) 'Comparing Curricula', *Review of Educational Research*, vol. 44, no. 1

Watson, J. D. (1972) *The Double Helix*, New York, Antheneum

Webb, E.J. *et al.* (1966) *Unobtrusive Measures: Nonreactive Research in the Social Sciences*, Chicago, Rand McNally

Welch, W. W. (1972) 'Curriculum Evaluation', *Review of Educational Research*, vol. 39, no. 4

Whitehead, A. N. (1929) *The Aims of Education*, New York, Macmillan Publishing Co.

Williams, C.T. and G. K. Wolfe (1979) *Elements of Research, A Guide for Writers*, Sherman Oaks, California, Alfred Publishing Co.

Wirt, F. M. and M. W. Kirst (1972) *Political and Social Foundations of Education*, Berkeley, California, McCutchan Publishing Co.

Wise, R. (1976) 'The Uses of Objectives in Curriculum Planning', *Curriculum Theory Network*, vol. 5, no. 4

Wittrock, M. C. and H.Cook (1975) 'Transfer of Prior Learning to Verbal Instruction', *AERJ*, vol. 12, no.2

Wulf, K. and B. Schave (1984) *Curriculum Design*, Glenview, Illinois, Scott Foresman and Co.

Index

ability level, 68
Aboriginal schools, 54
accreditation, 43
achievement, 96
achievement tests, 98
acting, 59
Adler, M., 24
adolescent identity, 66
adolescent needs, 42
adolescents, 83
affective, 47
affective development, 84
age grading, 46
Alexander, 12,14
Alexandria, 23
algebra, 22,23
almanac, 23
alternative program, 83 ff
alternative programs, 55
American Indian, 53 ff
American Revolution, 37
anatomy, 26
anthropology, 1,14,59
Apple, M., 38
application, 57
aptitude, 68,91,97
Aquinas, Thomas, 23,29
Arabic, 23
argument, 21
Aristotle, 20,21,23,24,57
arithmetic, 21,23,27,35
Arizona, 55
art, 48,59
arts, 34
Astrolabe, 23
astronomy, 21,23,28
astrophysicists, 34
attendance, mandatory, 4
attitude, 98,102
attitudes, 68
Australia, 54,59,61

Bacon, Francis, 26
Bantu schools, 54
Barzun, J., 52
basic skills, 97
Beauchamp, G., 13,32
behaviors, 14,17
behavioral problems, 83,86
behavioral sciences, 6,14
behavioralists, 42
beliefs, 60,61,71
Bernstein, R., 13
Bible, 24,29

Binet, A., 24,29
biochemistry, 34
biology, 34,38
Bobbitt, F., 39,48
Broudy, H., 24
Brownell, 12
Bruner, J., 35,54
Bureau of Indian Affairs, 54,55
bureaucracy, 53
bureaucracy, of school, 92
business practice, 92
Byron, 29

career education, 27
Carroll, Lewis, 96
cartographer, 90
cerebral palsy, 74,82
ceremony, 58
character, 27,38,45,46
character development, 49
Charles I, 24
checklist, 98,99
chemistry, 22,34,48
Chicago, 55
China, 23
Christians, 23
church, 24,28,36
civic training, 24,28,36
civics, 92
classroom management, 4
clerical speed, 64
cognitive, 47
cognitive skills, 92
cognitive tests, 98
Coleman Report, 101
Comenius, 28
communication skills, 68,73,86
community, 56,94,98
community support, 89
competence, 91
computer, 93
computer sciences, 34
Constantinople, 22
construct, personal, 47,49
construct, productive, 47,49
construct, social, 47,49
construction, 66 ff
contract schools, 55
Cooley W., 18,19
core curriculum, 7
course evaluation, 97
course of study, 97
criterion, 57
Cromwell, 24

116